SWU-800-008

UNIFORMS OF RUSSIAN ARMY DURING THE YEARS 1825-1855 VOL. 8

UNDER THE REIGN OF NICHOLAS I
EMPEROR OF RUSSIA BETWEEN 1825 TO 1855
GUARDS DRAGOONS, LANCERS, HUSSARS & OTHERS

From the Viskovatov's greatest work:
"Historical description of the clothing and
arms of the Russian Army"

English translation by Mark Conrad

SOLDIERSHOP PUBLISHING

AUTHOR
Aleksandr Vasilevich Viskovatov born 22 April (4 May New Style) 1804, died 27 February (11 March) 1858 in St. Petersburg, Russian military historian. He graduated from the 1st Cadet Corps and served in the artillery, the hydrographic depot of the Naval Ministry, and then in the Department of Military Educational Institutions. He mainly studied historical artifacts and the histories of military units. Viskovatov's greatest work was the Historical Description of the Clothing and Arms of the Russian Army.

PUBLISHING'S NOTE
None of **unpublished** images or text of our book may be reproduced in any format without the expressed written permission of Soldiershop.com when not indicate as marked with license creative commons 3.0 or 4.0. The publisher remains to disposition of the possible having right for all the doubtful sources images or not identifies. Our trademark: Soldiershop Publishing ©, The names of our series: Soldiers&Weapons, Battlefield, War in colour, PaperSoldiers, Soldiershop e-book etc. are herein © by Soldiershop.com.

NOTE ABOUT BOOK PRINTING BEFORE 1925
This book may contain text or images coming from a reproduction of a book published before 1925 (over seventy years ago). No effort has been made to modernize or standardize the spelling used in the original text, so this book may have occasional imperfections such as missing or blurred pages, poor pictures, errant marks, etc. that were either part of the original artifact, or were introduced by the scanning process. We believe this work is culturally important, and despite the imperfections, have elected to bring it back into print (digital and/or paper) as part of our continuing commitment to the preservation of printed works worldwide. We appreciate your understanding of the imperfections in the preservation process, and hope you enjoy this valuable book. Now this book is purpose re-built and is proof-read and re-type set from the original to provide an outstanding experience of reflowing text, also for an ebook reader. However Soldiershop publishing added, enriched, revised and overhauled the text, images, etc. of the cover and the book. Therefore, the job is now to all intents and purposes a derivative work, and the added, new and original parts of the book are the copyright of Soldiershop. On this second unpublished part of the book none of images or text may be reproduced in any format without the expressed written permission of Soldiershop. Almost many of the images of our books and prints are taken from original first edition prints or books that are no longer in copyright and are therefore public domain. We have been a specialized bookstore for a long time so we (and several friends antiquarian booksellers) have readily available a lot of ancient, historical and illustrated books not in copyright. Each of our prints, art designs or illustrations is either our own creation, or a fully digitally restoration by our computer artists, or non copyrighted images. All of our prints are "tagged" with a registered digital copyright. Soldiershop remains to disposition of the possible having right for all the doubtful sources images or not identifies.

LICENSES COMMONS
Much of the text in this book are from the *"Memoirs of the Empress Catherine II., by Catherine II, Empress of Russia"* This book is for the use of anyone anywhere at no cost and with almost no restrictions whatsoever. You may copy it, give it away or re-use it under the terms of the similar creative commons License. This book may utilize material marked with license creative commons 3.0 or 4.0 (CC BY 4.0), (CC BY-ND 4.0), (CC BY-SA 4.0) or (CC0 1.0). We give appropriate attribution credit and indicate if change were made below in the acknowledgements field.

ACKNOWLEDGEMENTS
A Special Thanks to NYPL and other institutions for their kindly permission to use some images of his archives, collections or books used in our book.

Title: **UNIFORMS OF RUSSIAN ARMY DURING THE YEARS 1825-1855. VOL. 8** -Under the reign of Nicholas I emperor of Russia between 1825-1855
By A.V.Viskovatov. Serie edit by Luca S. Cristini. First edition by Soldiershop. April 2019
Cover & Art Design: Luca S. Cristini. Plates re-colorations by Anna Cristini. ISBN code: 978-88-93274517
Published by Luca Cristini Editore, via Orio 35/4- 24050 Zanica (BG) ITALY. www.soldiershop.com

UNIFORMS
OF THE RUSSIAN ARMY
DURING THE YEARS
1825-1855
VOL. 8

UNDER THE REIGN OF NICHOLAS I EMPEROUR OF
RUSSIA BETWEEN 1825 AND 1855

*

GUARDS DRAGOONS, LANCERS, HUSSARS AND OTHERS

Portrait of the Emperor Nicholas I 1856 by Egor Ivanovich Botman

HISTORICAL DESCRIPTION OF THE CLOTHING AND ARMS OF THE RUSSIAN ARMY - A.V. VISKOVATOV
(First English translation by Mark Conrad)

Soldiershop is glad to presents the complete collection of the great job made by A.V. Viskovatov dedicated to the uniforms and weapons belonging from the first Zar and Russian emperors to the Russian army during the Napoleonic period, until 1860 about. The time we considered in this volume corresponds to the reigns of Nicholas I that was the Emperor of Russia from 1825 until 1855. He was also the King of Poland and Grand Duke of Finland. He is best known as a political conservative whose reign was marked by geographical expansion, repression of dissent, economic stagnation, poor administrative policies, a corrupt bureaucracy, and frequent wars that culminated in Russia's defeat in the Crimean War of 1853–56.

Our reprint in based on the original 19th century volumes. This part is distributed at now on six volumes.

Our new edition, the first ever published in English, both on paper and digital format, boasts a large number of color plates, many of them unpublished and re-coloured by our team of expert artists and scholars of uniformology. Each volume is based on 100 color plates or more, always accompanied by the original translated text which describes the subjets of the plates.

A unique work in its genre, a must have in any respecting collection!

Aleksandr Vasilevich Viskovatov born 22 April (4 May New Style) 1804, died 27 February (11 March) 1858 in St. Petersburg, Russian military historian. He graduated from the 1st Cadet Corps and served in the artillery, the hydrographic depot of the Naval Ministry, and then in the Department of Military Educational Institutions.

He mainly studied historical artifacts and the histories of military units. Viskovatov's greatest work was the Historical Description of the Clothing and Arms of the Russian Army (Vols. 1-30, St. Petersburg, 1841-62; 2nd ed. Vols. 1-34, St. Petersburg - Novosibirsk - Leningrad, 1899-1948). This work is based on a great quantity of archival documents and contains four thousand colored illustrations.

Viskovatov was the author of Chronicles of the Russian Army (Books 1-20, St. Petersburg, 1834-42) and Chronicles of the Russian Imperial Army (Parts 1-7, St. Petersburg, 1852). He collected valuable material on the history of the Russian navy which went into A Short Overview of Russian Naval Campaigns and General Voyages to the End of the XVII Century (St. Petersburg, 1864; 2nd edition Moscow, 1946). Together with A.I. Mikhailovskii-Danilevskii he helped prepare and create the Military Gallery in the Winter Palace.

He wrote the historical military inscriptions for the walls of the Hall of St. George in the Great Palace of the Kremlin. (From the article in the Soviet Military Encyclopedia.)

CONTENTS
*
Preface pag. 5

38 - Guards Dragoon Regiments. Pag. 7

39 - Guards Lancer Regiments. Pag. 11

40 - Guards Hussar Regiments. Pag. 14

41 - Life Guards Gendarmerie. Pag. 18

42 - Guards Train. Pag. 19

43 - Guards Foot Artillery. Pag. 22

44 - Guards Horse Artillery. Pag. 25

*

Notes pag. 28

Plates pag. 35

HISTORICAL DESCRIPTION OF THE CLOTHING AND ARMS OF THE RUSSIAN ARMY
Guards dragoons, lancers, hussars & others 1825-1855

CHANGES IN THE UNIFORMS AND EQUIPMENT OF TEMPORARY FORCES FROM 1801 TO 1825.

XXXVIII. GUARDS DRAGOON REGIMENTS. [*Gvardeiskie dragunskie polki.*]

11 February 1826 – Gray riding **trousers** with wide stripes were established for clerks and all non-combatant lower ranks of the L.-Gds. Dragoon and L.-Gds. Horse-Jäger Regiments [1].

10 June 1826 – Monograms and crowns on lower ranks' **saddlecloths** were ordered to be trimmed with yellow cord [2].

15 September 1826 – For lower ranks who served out the regulation number of years without reproach and who voluntarily remained on service there was established **gold galloon** to be worn on the left sleeve, as described above for the uniforms of other troops [3].

1 January 1827 - Small forged and stamped stars on officers' epaulettes were established to distinguish **rank**, as described above [4].

17 July 1827 – The L.-Gds. Horse-Jäger Regiment was ordered to exchange **horses** with the L.-Gds. Hussar Regiment, and by this means the regiment's horses became chestnuts [*gnedye*] [5].

31 July 1827 – Numbers and letters on **shako covers** were ordered to be painted in yellow oilpaint [6].

8 October 1827 – New pattern **sabers** were established, straighter than before, with a brass hilt, black grip, and iron scabbard [7].

13 October 1827 – The coats of lower combatant ranks were given **scale epaulettes** without fringe, the same color as the buttons, with a cloth backing and small cross straps the same color as the collar (Illus. 705). Along with this the field of officers' epaulettes was directed to be scaled [8].

10 November 1827 – Instead of slit cuffs, the L.-Gds. Dragoon Regiment was ordered to have **round cuffs** as in the infantry, with flaps the same color as the collar, each flap with three buttonhole loops, of yellow lace [*bason*] for lower ranks and gold for officers. **Piping** around the collar, cuffs, cuff flaps, and skirttail turnbacks was dark green (Illus. 705) [9].

14 December 1827 - The **lace** [*nashivka*] sewn onto lower ranks' left sleeves in the L.-Gds. Horse-Jäger Regiment, instituted on 15 September 1826, was ordered to be silver non-commissioned officers' galloon [10].

9 February 1828 – New pattern **shakos** were given, prescribed to be 5-1/2 vershoks [9-5/8 inches] high with an upper diameter not less than 5-5/8 vershoks [9-7/8 inches] or more than 6 vershoks [10-1/2 inches]. The upper lacquered edge was to be 5/16 vershok [1/2 inch] wide, with a pompon and cords that were the same color as the buttons for lower ranks but silver for officers. The plates on the shako remained as before (Illus. 706) [11].

24 April 1828 - Instead of the grey coats [*mundiry serago sveta*] previously used, all **non-combatant** non-commissioned officers were given dark-green **frock coats** with one row of buttons and the same collar, cuffs, and shoulder straps as for combatants, while the pants were grey with piping on the side seams in the same color as the collar. Instead of their previous coats [*mundiry*], non-combatant master-craftsmen lower ranks [*masterovye nestroevye nizhnie chiny*], as well as infirmary orderlies [*lazaretynye sluzhiteli*], were to wear jackets [*kurtki*] of grey cloth of the same pattern as the coat, while pants were to be as for the preceding non-combatants [12].

20 December 1828 – New pattern **shako plates** were confirmed (the same as established for guards infantry regiments on 24 April 1828): of red brass [copper] for the L.-Gds. Dragoon Regiment's lower ranks, as previously and gold for officers, and of white tin for L.-Gds. Horse-Jägers lower ranks (silver for officers) (Illus. 706 and 707) [13].

9 July 1829 - The wide stripes [*lampasy*] on officers' and lower ranks' **riding trousers** [*reituzy*] were removed, and only one row of piping was left on the side seams [14].

26 December 1829 - All combatant ranks were ordered to have uniform **buttons** with the raised image of a two-headed eagle [15].

24 April 1830 – Instead of their smocks [*kiteli*], lower combatant ranks were given dark-green **jackets** [*kurtki*] with the same collar and shoulder straps as on the dress coat, but without buttons on the collar [16].

24 September 1830 - The lining [*podkladka*] of officers' **frock coats** [*syurtuki*] was to be the same as the coat itself—dark green [17].

6 December 1831 – Lower ranks of the L.-Gds. Horse-Jäger Regiment, upon its inclusion in the Old Guard, were given **yellow lace** [*bason*] buttonhole loops for collars and cuffs, and the same lace was ordered to be sewn on the coats of trumpeters (Illus. 708) [18].

1 January 1832 - Generals who had **gold swords**, decorated with diamonds and with the inscription *"za khrabost"* [*"for courage"*], were ordered to wear these without swordknots [19].

10 January 1832 – In place of shakos, the L.-Gds. Horse-Grenadier Regiment, renamed from the L.-Gds. Dragoons, was given **helmets** of black lacquered leather with two peaks and a standing front plate, and over the helmet a crossways plume of horse hair trimmed into a round shape, red for trumpeters and black for other ranks. There was an edging on the front peak and grenades on the sides, under [sic – should be "over"] the scales, of red brass (gilded for officers), along with the previous shako plate. When in formation and during parades a red cloth flap was fastened to the upper part of the helmet body behind the plume. The cloth was 4 vershoks [7 inches] wide, 12-1/2 vershoks [21-7/8 inches] long, and was rounded at its lower end. Along its edges and down its center was sewn yellow woolen lace 1/2 vershok [7/8 inch] wide (gold for officers). Hanging fringe was introduced for lower ranks' **scaled epaulettes** (similar to that for field-grade officers), of red wool, and they were also given lancer pattern **girdles** with a dark-green middle and piping along the edges the same color as the collar (Illus. 709 and 710) [20].

1 September 1832 – All combatant non-commissioned officers were given **muskets**, and trumpeters and drummers were introduced into the regiment (Illus. 711) [21].

3 April 1833 – The L.-Gds. Horse-Jäger Regiment, upon being renamed the L.-Gds. Dragoons, was prescribed **dragoon weapons** [22].

24 December 1833 – Lower non-combatant ranks, instead of deerskin **sword belts**, were ordered to have these of red Russian leather with a frog for the bayonet scabbard. Along with this the L.-Gds. Dragoon Regiment was ordered to have round infantry **cuffs**, with the cuff flaps to be red with three yellow buttonhole loops (silver for officers) on each, and with dark-green piping on the cuffs and flaps. On this same date lower ranks were given **girdles** identical to those introduced on 10 January 1832 for the L.-Gds. Horse-Grenadier Regiment. (Illus. 712) [23].

6 April 1834 – **Muskets** were ordered to be carried not in small buckets [*bushmaty*], but over the shoulder on a strap of a newly confirmed pattern. Consequent to this the former buckets were removed from saddles (Illus. 713) [24].

13 April 1834 – **Cartridge pouches** and **cross straps** were established, of a new pattern with a smaller pouch lid and and a narrower strap [25].

2 May 1834 – In order to improve handling of the **saber**, its hilt was ordered to be remade according to a new pattern, as in army dragoon regiments [26].

30 June 1834 – On **muskets** the small lower handles [*antabki*] for the cross strap were ordered to be held by small screws. Additionally, special brackets with a threaded screw were to be made for fastening the handles to the butt [27].

3 December 1834 – **Pistols** were withdrawn [28].

7 December 1834 – **Shako cords** in the L.-Gds. Dragoon Regiment were ordered to no longer reach to the waist, but only halfway down the back [29].

15 January 1835 – The mounted non-commissioned officers in the L.-Gds. Dragoon Regiment's lancer squadron [*pikernyi eskadron*] were prescribed one **pistol** each [30].

13 April 1835 – When in formation, officers of the L.-Gds. Dragoon Regiment were ordered to use a toggle to fasten one end of the **shako cord** to a loop made behind the shako using the cord itself, and at all other times, when obliged to take off the shako, this cord was to be detached from the loop, whereupon it was left around the neck with its slide, which was to be in back at the middle of the neck, and the end with the toggle was to be fastened to the second coat button from the top so that the cord passed under the right arm and over the pouch belt (Illus. 714) [31].

22 November 1835 – For greater convenience when riding, the **copper kettles** were ordered to be strapped to the right side of the valises and not to the left [32].

31 January 1836 – Nine **buttons** were prescribed for lower ranks' greatcoats in the L.-Gds. Horse-Grenadier Regiment: six down the front, 3 on the shoulder straps, and 1 behind on the flaps. In the L.-Gds. Dragoons—11 buttons: 6 down the front, on the collar tabs, 2 on the shoulder straps, and 1 behind on the flap [33].

27 April 1836 – **Pompons** in the L.-Gds. Dragoon Regiment were ordered to be backed with black leather [34].

5 May 1836 – New pattern **sword belts** were introduced in both regiments, with slings and a strap with a small hook. The slings and strap were not movable, but sewn firmly to the sword belt [35].

13 May 1836 - Officers' **saddle girths** [*podprugi*] were to be dark green with red stripes [36].

9 October 1836 - As a place for their pistols, staff-trumpeters, trumpeters, and drummers [*shtab-trubachi, trubachi i bara-*

banshchiki] were to have **holders** [*chushki*], fitted to the saddle over the saddlecloth: on the left side for trumpeters and on the right for drummers. For cartridges they were to have **cartridge pouches** [*lyadunki*] with crossbelts, as for the other lower ranks (Illus. 715) [37].

17 January 1837 - When wearing the **frock coat** without the sash, generals and field and company-grade officers were ordered to wear the **saber** under the frock, attaching the upper ring to the hook next to the first sling and putting the hilt through an specially made pocket, as in the Infantry. When wearing the frock coat with the sash, however, the saber was to be over the coat, left free on its slings and not hung onto the hook [38].

14 February 1837 - Staff-trumpeters, trumpeters, and drummers who were prescribed pistols when in mounted formation and—for cartridges—pouches with belts, were also to wear these **cartridge pouches** when in dismounted formation [39].

16 July 1837 - The new pattern of officers' **sash** was confirmed, identical with that described above for Grenadier regiments [40].

17 December 1837 - In order to introduce uniformity in the style of officers' **epaulettes**, confirmation was given to a pattern with an additional, fourth, twist of narrow braid [41].

11 January 1838 - Approval was given to a description of the officer's **saddle**, in agreement in all details with that presented above for Army Dragoon regiments [42].

23 February 1838 - Regulations were confirmed concerning the **pistol holders** [*pistoletnyya chushki*] on the saddle (see Army Dragoon regiments) [43].

12 March 1838 - A new pattern of **bandolier belt** [*pantalernyi remen'*] was confirmed for landers in the L.-Gds. Dragoon Regiment, longer than the cartridge-pouch crossbelt [*lyadunochnaya perevyaz'*] and in complete agreement with the description presented above for Guards Cuirassier regiments [44].

4 January 1839 - The **pants** of generals and field and company-grade officers were not to have any bows or bands in front [*speredi bantov ne imet*] but rather worn completely plain [*gladkii*], as by lower ranks [45].

16 October 1840 - The regulation concerning lower ranks' **chevrons** [*shevrony*] was confirmed (see Grenadier regiments) [46].

23 January 1841 - The capes [*bolshie vorotniki*] of officers' **greatcoats** were to be 1 arshin [28 inches] long as measured from the bottom edge of the collar [47].

13 November 1842 - All combatant ranks were given a new pattern **saber** [*sablya*], with a bayonet sheath [*shtykovye nozhny*] for lower ranks (Illus. 716 and 717) [48].

8 April 1843 – The L.-Gds. Dragoon Regiment was given new **shakos**, lower than previously and slighty tapered towards the bottom (Illus. 718) [49]. Along with this, in order to distinguish **rank** among the lower ranks, in both regiments lace [*nashivki*] was established to be sewn onto coat epaulettes and greatcoat shoulder straps just as in Army Dragoon regiments, but of guards tape and galloon [*gvardeiskii bason i galun*] the same color as the buttons.

10 May 1843 - Cover flaps [*kryshki*] for **cartridge pouches** were to be (with the cover sewn to the box): 4-1/2 vershoks [8 inches] long, 4-7/8 vershoks [9 inches] wide at the top edge, and 5-5/8 vershoks [10 inches] wide along the bottom edge [50].

2 January 1844 - Officers were to have a **cockade** on the band of the forage cap [51].

9 May 1844 – In the L.-Gds. Dragoon Regiment shakos were replaced by **helmets** [*kaski*] with plumes [*sultany*]—red for trumpeters and black for other ranks—of the same pattern and in accordance with the same directives as for Guards infantry regiments at this time, but with the addition of a metal edging [*obodok*] on the front peak, of the same color as the helmet mountings (Illus. 719 and 720) [52].

20 May 1844 – Piping around the top of the **forage cap** was established to be red in the 1st Double-Squadrons [*diviziony*], white in the 2nd, blue [*svetlosinii*] in the 3rd, and dark green in reserve and replacement double-squadrons [53].

21 September 1844 - **Non-commissioned officer standard-bearers** [*shtandartnye unter-ofitsery*] in formation were ordered to always have the cartridge pouch under the crossbelt for the standard [54].

17 December 1844 – Instead of undress coats and hats [*vitsmundiry*], combatant field and company-grade officers in the L.-Gds. Horse-Grenadier Regiment were to wear **helmets**: with the rear length of cloth [*lopast'*] when in dress coats [*mundiry*], and without when in frock coats [*syurtuki*] [55].

4 January 1845 - Officers' **helmets** in the L.-Gds. Dragoon Regiment were to have a cockade on the right side under the chin-scales (Illus. 721) [56].

15 November 1845 - The regiments were to have **pioneer axes** [*shantsovye topory*], two for each platoon [*vzvod*]. Additionally, there were to be 56 iron **spades** [*lopaty*] in each regiment, as referred to above for Cuirassier regiments [57].

30 April 1846 – Officers in the L.-Gds. Horse-Grenadier Regiment were ordered to wear, when not on duty, helmet **chinscales** of the pattern for other troops, fastening them above the visor [58].

5 July 1846 – Helmet **chinscales** were ordered to be fastened over the rear peak (Illus. 722) [59].

7 August 1846 – In connection with the introduction of **percussion firearms** in the Guards cavalry, confirmation was given to the following description of fitting firing-cap pouches [*kapsyul'nye sumochki*] and stowing the tin case [*zhestyanoi futlyar*], small valise [*chemodanchik*], and piston screwdriver [*pistonnaya otverka*]:

a) Firing-cap pouches were to be lined inside with fur with the nap facing downwards, so that the firing-caps could not slip out under rough shaking. The pouches were to be fitted to the right side of the chest and fastened to the cartridge-pouch belt so that the cap pouch's lower edge was even with the coat's fourth button from the bottom. The small strap of hard leather for fastening these pouches was to be wider than in the infantry and on two buttons. The pouch cover was to be bent over using the strap so that its end was bent under and did not hang out.

b) Tin cases for protecting the firing caps were to be stowed in the valise on the right side.

c) Small valises with the soldier's toilet articles were to be of cloth of the same color as prescribed for the regimental uniform, and stowed in the left pistol carrier.

d) Piston screwdrivers were to be stowed under the cover of the cartridge pouch [*podsumok*] [60].

13 September 1846 - Officers' **pistols** were to be of a new pattern with a percussion lock [*udarnye zamki*], for which new carriers [*kobury*] were approved (see Army Cuirassier regiments) [61].

19 May 1847 – Lower non-combatant ranks were prescribed the same **forage caps** as in Guards Infantry regiments [62].

31 August 1847 - Under all circumstances in which lower ranks of Dragoon regiments previously were directed to wear their **greatcoats** thrown back [*v-nakidku*], they were now ordered to wear them using the sleeves, over any personal equipment, and open [*v-raspashku*] [63].

5 November 1847 - **Greatcoats** worn using the sleeves, open and over accouterments, were ordered to be worn only in mounted order. However, the wearing of greatcoats in dismounted order was left according to the previous manner [64].

9 January 1848 – Generals, and field and company-grade officers, on those days when after guard mount [*posle razvoda*] they had to remain in holiday uniform [*prazdnichnaya forma*], were allowed to wear, for walking out [*dlya progulok*], **frock coats** with *chakchiry* pants, along with **helmets**: with the back cloth in the L.-Gds. Horse-Grenadier Regiment, and with the plume in the L.-Gds. Dragoons [65].

19 January 1848 - With the introduction of officers' pistols with percussion locks, confirmation was given to the description of the **firing-cap pouch** [*kapsyulnaya sumochka*] worn with the cartridge pouch (see Army Cuirassier regiments) [66].

24 January 1848 - Deerskin **swordbelts** [*losinnyya portupei*] were introduced in both regiments, following the pattern used in His Royal Highness the Crown Prince of Württemberg's Dragoon Regiment, to be worn over the shoulder and on top of the coat and frock coat (Illus. 723) [67].

20 February 1848 - For officers these **swordbelts** were to be of gold galloon on black leather for the L.-Gds. Horse-Grenadier Regiment, and of silver galloon on black leather for the L.-Gds. Dragoons (Illus. 724) [68].

25 April 1848 - The **valise's** flap with buttons was removed [69].

24 December 1849 - The grips of **gold swords** awarded for bravery were prescribed to be gold [70].

5 March 1850 - **Bandoliers** for standards were established to to be 2-1/2 arshins [4-3/8 inches] wide, 2 arshins [4-1/2 feet] long, and lined on the outer side with green velvet: with gold fringe, galloon, and hook with brackets in the L.-Gds. Horse-Grenadier Regiment, but silver in the L.-Gds. Dragoons. The inner side was to be lined with red cloth [71].

30 March 1851 - With the introduction of smaller **bandoliers** [*pantalery*] and crossbelts with a movable **firing-cap pouch** [*perevyazi s peredvizhnoyu kapsyulnoyu sumochkoyu*] fitted onto a small iron hook, approval was given to a description of them (see Army Cuirassier regiments) [72].

15 April 1851 - Approval was given to a description for fitting straps to the **valise** for dismounted lower ranks in che Cavalry. This was also prescribed to be in effect for personnel released on leave from Cavalry units (see Army Cuirassier regiments) [73].

3 January 1852 - The cases or coverings [*chekhly, ili nakladki*] introduced for Army Infantry on 8 July 1851 for the **firing nipples** [*sterzhni*] of percussion weapons were ordered to be used in the Cavalry [74].

26 July 1852 The gray **forage caps** of non-combatant lower ranks were given a band the same color as the collar of combatant ranks [75].

15 November 1853 – In the Guards Cavalry it was ordered to adopt the descriptions presented above under Army Cuirassier regiments for: rolling **greatcoats** on saddles and officers' light-cavalry **horse furniture**, as well as the list of **items** which a cavalry soldier was to have when on campaign and at inspections, and the description of sundry articles and the directions on where to stow them [76].

29 April 1854 - During wartime, generals and field and company-grade officers were to have **campaign greatcoats** (see Grenadier regiments) [77].

XXXIX. GUARDS LANCER REGIMENTS. [*Gvardeiskie ulanskie polki*].

11 February 1826 – Gray **riding trousers** [*reituzy*] with stripes [*lampasy*] were established for clerks [*pisarya*] and all non-combatant lower ranks [78].

10 July 1826 – Monograms and crowns on lower ranks' **saddlecloths** were ordered to be trimmed as follows: with yellow cord in the L.-Gds. Lancer Regiment (Illus. 725), and with white in H.I.H. THE HEIR AND TESAREVICH CONSTANTINE PAVLOVICH'S L.-Gds. Lancers [79].

15 September 1826 - Lower ranks who had served out the regulation number of years without reproach and who voluntarily remained in service were ordered to wear **gold galloon** [*nashivka iz zolotago galuna*] sewn onto the left sleeve, as related above for other troops [80].

1 January 1827 - In order to distinguish rank, it was ordered that officers' **epaulettes** were to have small forged and stamped stars of the same appearance and according to the same scheme as for the preceding Cavalry regiments [81].

31 July 1827 - Numbers and letters on **headdress covers** [*chekhly shapok*] were directed to be in yellow oil paints [82].

8 October 1827 – A new patter **saber** was confirmed, with a brass hilt, black grip, and iron scabbard, straighter than before, as described above for Army Dragoon regiments (Illus. 726) [83].

13 October 1827 – Instead of woolen epaulettes with fringes on their jackets, combatant lower ranks were given **scaled epaulettes** [*cheshuichatye epolety*] without fringes, the same color as their buttons and with a cloth backing and small cross strap the same color as collar (Illus. 726). Along with this, the field on officers' epaulettes was directed to also be scaled [84].

14 December 1827 – The **lace** [*nashivka*] sewn onto lower ranks' left sleeves, instituted on 15 September 1826, was ordered to be gold in the L.-Gds. Lancer Regiment, and silver in H.I.H. TESAREVICH CONSTANTINE PAVLOVICH'S L.-Gds. Lancers, in both cases of the non-commissioned officers' galloon prescribed for that regiment in which the man who had served the regulation time for retirement was voluntarily remaining in service. In this same year H.I.H. TSESAREVICH CONSTANTINE PAVLOVICH'S L.-Gds. Lancer Regiment was allowed to have black sheep's fleece **saddlecloths** instead of cloth ones (Illus. 727) [85].

26 January 1828 - For officers' headdresses, the small chain [*tsepochka*] on the **chinstrap** [*podborodnyi remen*] was replaced by standard shako chinstrap scales the same color as the buttons (Illus. 728) [86].

24 March 1828 – It was forbidden for the uniform **jackets** of lower ranks to have cinches [*peretyazhki*] [87].

24 April 1828 – Instead of gray coats, all **non-combatant** non-commissioned officers were given dark-green single-breasted **frock coats** [*syurtuki*] with the same collar, cuffs, and shoulder straps as for combatants, while pants were to be gray with red piping in the side seams. For master craftsmen [*masterovye nizhnie chiny*], as well as lazaret orderlies [*lazaretnye sluzhiteli*], in place of the coat, gray cloth jackets [*kurtki*] were established, of the same pattern as the coat, and also pants as for the preceding non-combatants [88].

9 July 1829 – The wide stripes on officers' and lower ranks' **riding trousers** were removed, leaving only piping on the side seams [89].

26 December 1829 - All combatant ranks were ordered to have uniform **buttons** with the raised image of a two-headed eagle, as prescribed for the full-dress headdress plate [90].

24 April 1830 – Instead of smocks [*kiteli*] for combatant lower ranks, dark-green **jackets** [*kurtki*] were established, with likewise dark-green collar, cuffs, and shoulder straps, with red piping on the collar, cuffs, and shoulder straps and the buttons prescribed for full-dress jackets [91].

24 September 1830 - The lining [*podkladka*] of officers' **frock coats** was to be the same color as the coat itself—very dark blue [*temnosinii*] [92].

6 December 1831 – For H.I.H. GRAND DUKE MICHAEL PAVLOVICH'S L.-Gds. Lancer Regiment, renamed from H.I.H. TSAREVICH CONSTANTINE PAVLOVICH'S Lancers, instead of black fleece **saddlecloths**, there were established new ones of very dark-blue cloth, with the cloth lining and other fittings remaining as before (Illus. 729) [93].

1 January 1832 – Generals with **gold sabers** decorated with diamonds and inscribed "*For Courage*" were ordered to wear these without sword knots [94].

22 February 1833 – Officers were allowed to have riding **horses** with long tails [95].

15 April 1834 – **Cartridge pouches** and **crossbelts** of new patterns were established, with smaller cover flaps and narrower crossbelt [96].

2 May 1834 - In order that **sabers** [*sabli*] might be better handled, it was ordered that their hilts [*yefesy*] be reworked according to a new pattern, as explained above in detail for the uniforms and weapons of Army Dragoon regiments [97].

3 December 1834 – **Pistols** were introduced into both regiments, to be worn on a man's person in a special holder [*chushka*] [98].

15 January 1835 - As a supplement to the above directive of 3 December 1834, all mounted trumpeters, non-commissioned officers, and privates were prescribed to have one **pistol** each [99].

19 July 1835 - To carry the pistol, it was ordered to have a **holder** [*chushka*] on the left side of the swordbelt [*portupeya*], as set forth above for Army Dragoon regiments (Illus. 730) [100].

31 January 1836 - Lower ranks' **greatcoats** were to have nine buttons instead of ten: six down the front opening, two on the shoulder straps, and one behind on the flaps [101].

9 October 1836 - As a place for their pistols, staff-trumpeters and trumpeters [*shtab-trubachi i trubachi*] were to have **holders** [*chushki*] of a special pattern, fitted to the saddle on the left side over the saddlecloth. For cartridges they were to have **cartridge pouches** [*lyadunki*] with crossbelts, as for other lower ranks (Illus. 731) [102].

17 January 1837 – General and field and company-grade officers, when in **frock coats** without sashes, were ordered to wear the **saber** under the frock coat, with the upper ring fastened to a hook on the first sling and passing the hilt through a pocket specially made for this purpose, in the same way as half-sabers and swords were worn in the infantry. When in frock coats with the sash, the saber was to be worn over the coat without being placed on the hook, but rather hanging loose on the slings [103].

14 February 1837 - Staff-trumpeters and trumpeters, who were prescribed pistols when in mounted formation and, for their cartridges, **cartridge pouches** [*lyadunki*] with belts, were ordered to also wear these cartridgepouches when in dismounted formation [104].

11 March 1837 – New pattern **carbines** [*karabiny*] were introduced in both regiments, of the same pattern as those introduced at this time in Army Dragoon and Hussar regiments (Illus. 732) [105].

13 July 1837 - With the introduction of new-pattern carbines in both regiments, the **swordbelts** for the carrying of sabers while in dismounted formation were directed to have brass hooks on straps with brass buckles, following the pattern for hussar swordbelts [106].

15 July 1837 - A new pattern of officers' **sash** [*sharf*] was approved, identical with that described above for Grenadier regiments [107].

14 August 1837 - Officers and lower ranks in formation were ordered to not pass their **headdress cords** [*etishkety*] under the epaulette, but simply wear them around the neck so that they hang to the middle of the back and fasten to the button on the headdress. Officers not in formation, and lower ranks in half-dress uniform [*poluforma*] were directed to wear the cords as before, passing them under the epaulette on the right shoulder [108].

17 December 1837 - A new pattern of officers' **epaulettes** was confirmed, identical with that introduced at this time in Dragoon regiments, i.e. with an additional, fourth, row of narrow cord [109].

11 January 1838 - Approval was given to a description of the officer's **saddle** which was prescribed for use on 6 March 1834, in agreement in all details with those presented above for Army Dragoon regiments [110].

23 February 1838 - Regulations were confirmed concerning the **pistol holders** [*pistoletnyya chushki*] established for the saddle on 9 October 1836, as set forth above in detail for Army Dragoon regiments [111].

On this same date confirmation was given to the following description of fitting **lancer headdress cords** [*ulanskii etishket*]: Both ends of the line [*snur*], to which are sewn tassels above large slides [*varvorki*], are sewn together for 1/2 inch and this is attached to the left lapel's upper button, under the epaulette. Then the double line is passed under the epaulette between the small cross strap and collar and tied behind the epaulette with a small slide. From the slide one line encircles the collar from the front and then meets with the other line directly behind the collar. At this point the line is caught by two small slides 1 inch apart from each other, and then it is either fastened to the headdress or let down from the collar as a festoon about 1/3 of the way down the back, and passes between the cross strap and button of the first epaulette and, finally, falls from the right side between the sleeve and lapel, fastened to the lapel's upper button, under it. But when the lapels are closed, then the upper two slide knots must pass under the epaulette between the cross strap and collar. A thin cord about 8 vershoks [14 inches] long is tied to the upper end of the epaulette. A thin cord is tied to the upper end of the epaulette, about 14 inches long. On the coat, on the collar's lower seam, where the top of the epaulette should be, two reinforced holes [*obmetannyya diry*] are made, into which the ends of the thin cord are inserted and tied together on the inside, Small cross straps are sewn onto the shoulders: on the right shoulder both ends are sewn fast, but on the left shoulder the front end of this small strap is sewn fast while a small metal loop is sewn onto the other end. A loop of thread [*nityanaya petlya*] is made on the coat and from it, under the middle of the epaulette on the coat, is sewn a small wire hook. The small strap, going over the epaulette, is passed through the thread loop and fastened to this hook.

4 January 1839 - The **riding-trousers** [*reituzy*] and **chakchiry** pants of generals and field and company-grade officers were not to have any bows or bands in front [*speredi bantov ne imet'*] but rather worn completely plain [*gladkii*] in the manner prescribed for lower ranks [112].

16 October 1840 – Lower ranks who had received the right to indefinite leave after serving out the time required for retirement yet voluntarily remained on service were ordered to be given sewn-on **chevrons** for their subsequenty service, of gold or silver galoon, to be worn on the left sleeve, one for every five years. On this same basis chevrons were prescribed for non-commissioned officers who declined promotion to officer rank and were receiving two-thirds of an ensign's pay, the chevrons being authorized for five or more years of service after declining promotion [113].

23 January 1841 - The capes [*bolshie vorotniki*] of officers' **greatcoats** were to be 1 arshin [28 inches] long as measured from the bottom edge of the collar [114].

31 January 1843 - The **lances** [*piki*] in both regiments were ordered to be reworked according to the new pattern, so that with its shaft [*drevko*] and spearhead [*nakonechnik*] it measured 4 arshins [10 ½ feet] [115].

8 April 1843 - In order to distinguish rank among the lower ranks, **lace** [*nashivki*] was to be sewn onto jacket epaulettes and greatcoat shoulder straps according to the scheme prescribed for Army Dragoon regiments, except that Guards galloon was substituted for Army pattern [116].

10 May 1843 – Dimensions for the cover flaps [*kryshki*] of **cartridge pouches** [*lyadunki*] were laid down as (with the cover sewn to the box): 4-1/2 vershoks [8 inches] long, 4-7/8 vershoks [9 inches] wide at the top edge, and 5-5/8 vershoks [10 inches] wide along the bottom edge. The oval **belt rings** for carbines were to be replaced with circular ones. Belts were attached to the stocks [*lozhi*] of the carbines by means of special straps with buckles, and in order to avoid the upper brass band hitting the spurs, as well as so that the carbines would not drag on the ground when dismounted, they were to be raised up by shortening the bandolier, according to the height of the individual [117].

2 January 1844 - Officers were to have a **cockade** on the cap band of the forage cap, as related above in detail for Grenadier regiments [118].

19 February 1844 - The shortening of the **bandolier** as established on 10 May 1843, in accordance with an individual's height, was to be done by means of a brass buckle on its end, so that below it was even with the lower edge of the jacket (Illus. 734) [119].

1844 May 20 - A new scheme for the various **forage caps** of lower ranks was confirmed, based on which they remained very dark blue as before, while the piping around the top was to be: in the 1st double-squadron [*divizion*] — red, in the 2nd — white, in the 3rd — light blue, and in the replacement [*zapasnyi*] and reserve [*rezervnyi*] squadrons — dark green. The cap band was prescribed to be the same color as the full-dress headdress, with two very dark-blue pipings around both edges, and with the cut-out number of the squadron or [sic, should be "and"] the Cyrillic letter Е [for *eskadron* — M.C.]. When the cap band was yellow, the numeral and letter were to be on red cloth, and when ren, then the numeral and leter were to be on yellow cloth. For officers of all double-squadrons the cap band was the same as the lower ranks', with two dark-green pipings, but without numerals or letters, while the piping around the top of the forage cap was red [120].

21 September 1844 - **Non-commissioned officer standard-bearers** [*shtandartnye unter-ofitsery*] in formation were ordered to always have the cartridge pouch under the standard's crossbelt [121].

19 November 1845 - On the **lances**, the clamps [*skoby*] which came out of the sharp upper end and blunt lower end to hold them to the shaft, as well as the small "ears" in which the lance sling [*temlyak*] went, were to be painted the same color as the shafts, as was done on the lances of the previous pattern [122].

7 August 1846 – The confirmed description of how to fit **firing-cap pouches** [*kapsyul'nye sumochki*] and stow the tin case [*zhestyanoi futlyar*], small valise [*chemodanchik*], and piston screwdriver [*pistonnaya otverka*], presented in detail for Guards Dragoon regiments, also applied to Guards Lancer regiments with the difference that in the latter the firing-cap pouches were fastened not to the right side of the chest but to the left, 1-1/2 vershoks [2-5/8 inches] below the epaulette (Illus. 735) [123].

13 September 1846 - New carriers [*kobury*] for officer's percussion **pistols** were approved as for Army Cuirassier regiments [124].

19 May 1847 – A description of forage caps for noncombatant lower ranks was confirmed (see Guards heavy infantry regiments) [125].

9 January 1848 - Field and company-grade officers, on those days when holiday uniform [*prazdnichnaya forma*] was prescribed after guard mount [*posle razvoda*], were allowed to wear, for walking out [*dlya progulok*], **frock coats** with *chakchiry* pants [126].

19 January 1848 – A description of the firing-cap pouch for officers' cartridge pouches was confirmed as for Army Cuirassier regiments [127].

25 April 1848 - The **valise's flap** [*klapan na chemodane*] with buttons was done away with [128].

7 November 1849 - **Pompons** were ordered to be 5-5/8 vershoks [10 inches] in circumference [129].

24 December 1849 - The grips of the hilts of **gold swords** awarded for bravery were to be gold [130].

8 March 1850 - **Bandoliers** for standards were ordered to be 2-1/2 vershoks [4-3/8] inches wide, 2 arshins [4-1/2 feet] long, and lined with as follows: in the L.-Gds. Lancers, on the outside—with red velvet and gold fringe, gallon, and hook with brackets, and in H.H. the Heir and Tsesarevich's L.-Gds. Lancers—with yellow velvet with silver appointments, and on the inside with red for the first regiment and with yellow for the second [131].

3 February 1851 - **Covers** [*chekhly*] for lower ranks' headdresses were established. The back half was to fasten to the front one so that the chin scales could be worn on the visor, in the style of officers. The rear piece was folded up inside the cover [132].

30 March 1851 – With. the introduction of smaller **bandoliers** [*pantalery*] and **crossbelts** with a movable firing-cap pouch [*perevyazi s peredvizhnoyu kapsyulnoyu sumochkoyu*], approval was given to their description as presented above in detail for Army Cuirassier regiments [133].

15 April 1851 - Approval was given to a description for fitting straps to the **valise** for dismounted lower ranks and personnel released on leave (see Army Cuirassier regiments) [134].

3 January 1852 - Cases or coverings [*chekhly, ili nakladki*] for the **firing nipples** [*sterzhni*] of percussion weapons were introduced, as established for Army Infantry on 8 July 1856 [135].

26 January 1852 – The band on noncombatants' forage caps was prescribed to be the same color as the coat collar of combatant ranks [136].

16 July 1852 - Covers for the **firing nipples** of percussion weapons were established in accordance with the description confirmed for Cuirassier regiments [137].

13 August 1853 - Generals and field and company-grade officers, when in campaign uniform [*pokhodnaya forma*] of **frock coat** without sash, were directed to buckle the **swordbelt** over the coat [138].

18 February 1854 - The regulation of 15 November 1853 concerning light-cavalry **horse furniture**, presented above in the section for Army Cuirassier regiments, was also extended to Guards Lancer regiments [139].

29 April 1854 - During wartime, generals and field and company-grade officers were to have **campaign greatcoats** [*pokhodnyya shineli*] of the same color and pattern as the greatcoats of lower ranks. With the greatcoats it was prescribed that there be worn sword belts and pouch belts of their prescribed gold or silver galloon, while headdress cords and sashes were not to worn [140].

XL. GUARDS HUSSAR REGIMENTS. [*Gvardeiskie gusarskie polki*].

11 February 1826 – Gray **riding trousers** [*reituzy*] with stripes [*lampasy*] were established for clerks [*pisarya*] and in general all non-combatant lower ranks. At the beginning of this year there was a change in the embroidery on officers' **sabertaches** and **saddlecloths** in the L.-Gds. Hussar Regiment (Illus. 736 and 737) [141].

10 June 1826 – The L.-Gds. Hussar Regiment was given new-pattern **shakos** of the style used by the L.-Gds. Grodno Hussars since 1824 and by Army Hussar regiments since 25 November 1826, but keeping the previous colors and appointments. Instead of the previous dark-blue **collars and cuffs** the regiment was prescribed red, the same color as the dolman (Illus. 738 and 739). Along with this, in both this regiment and the L.-Gds. Grodno Hussars, officers when in the undress coat [*vitsemundir*] were ordered to wear dark-green long **pants** with galloon on the side seams in the same color as the buttons (Illus. 740) [142].

15 September 1826 - Lower ranks who had served out the regulation number of years without reproach and who voluntarily remained on service were ordered to wear **gold galloon** sewn onto the left sleeve, as related above in detail for Cuirassier regiments [143].

1 January 1827 - In order to distinguish rank, it was ordered that officers' **epaulettes** (on the undress coat) were to have small forged and stamped stars of the same appearance and according to the same scheme as related above (see the preceding forces) [144].

17 February 1827 - Officers' **girdles** [*poyasy*] were directed to have a mixture of black and orange silk [145].

17 July 1827 – The L.-Gds. Hussar Regiment was ordered to **exchange horses** with the L.-Gds. Horse-Jägers, and in this way the established color for horses in the regiment became gray [146].

22 July 1827 – In the L.-Gds. Hussar Regiment, instead of cloaks [*plashchi*] it was ordered to have **greatcoats** [*shineli*] with collars and cuffs of red (Illus. 741) [147].

31 July 1827 - Numbers and letters on **shako covers** [*kivernye chekhly*] were ordered to be in yellow oil paints [148].

13 October 1827 - On their undress coats, generals and field and company-grade officers were to have **epaulettes** with a scaled field [*epolety s cheshuichatym polem*], as established at this time for the L.-Gds. Dragoon and L.-Gds. Horse-Jäger regiments [149].

14 December 1827 - The **lace** [*nashivka*] sewn onto lower ranks' left sleeves, instituted on 15 September 1826, was ordered to be gold in the L.-Gds. Hussar Regiment and silver in the L.-Gds. Grodno Hussars, of the non-commissioned officer's galloon of that regiment in which the man served out the prescribed period and voluntarily remained in service [150].

24 April 1828 – There were the same changes in uniforms for **noncombatant** non-commissioned officers and lower ranks as described above (see the L.-Gds. Horse-Grenadier Regiment) [151].

9 July 1828 – The wide stripes were ordered removed from the **riding trousers** of officers and lower ranks, leaving only piping on the side seams [152].

26 December 1828 – For all ranks there were established uniform **buttons** with the raised image of a two-headed eagle, as prescribed for the shako plate [153].

1 January 1832 - Generals possessing **gold sabers** decorated with diamonds and inscribed "*Za khrabost*" ["*For courage*"] were ordered to wear these without swordknots [154].

15 January 1832 – Instead of **olive-colored** uniforms and saddlecloths, **green** cloth was established for the L.-Gds. Grodno Hussars. Along with this the existing fleece saddlecloths in this regiment were withdrawn (Illus. 742) [155].

27 February 1833 – Crimson [*alyi*] was established as the color for pelisses and dolmans; shakos, *chakchiry* pants and sabertaches were light blue [*svetlosinii*]—all with white appointments. Girdles were white with light blue slides; saddlecloths were light blue with white toothed edging and thin red cord. Valises were light blue (Illus. 743 and 744). Along with this change, light-blue collars, cuffs, piping, and skirt lining were prescribed for **officers undress coats** (Illus. 745). The same piping was prescribed for officers frock coats. **Greatcoat** collars were to be crimson with a light-blue tab on each side, with a white button; shoulder straps were to be light blue with red piping. **Jackets** were light blue with the same color for the collar and cuffs, and on them—red piping (Illus. 745) [156].

13 April 1834 - **Cartridge pouches** [*lyadunki*] and **crossbelts** [*perevyazi*] were to be of a new pattern, with smaller-sized cover flaps [*kryshki*] and narrower crossbelts [157].

2 May 1834 - In order that **sabers** [*sabli*] might be better handled, it was ordered that their hilts [*yefesy*] be reworked according to a new pattern, as described above in detail for the L.-Gds. Horse-Grenadier Regiment) [158].

3 December 1834 - **Pistols** were withdrawn from both regiments [159].

7 December 1834 - Lines to the **shako** (when this was being worn) were not to reach to the waist, as before, but only halfway down the back [160].

15 January 1835– Mounted non-commissioned officers were ordered to each have one **pistol** [161].

20 February 1835 - With the withdrawal of pistols from both regiments, the **ramrods** [*shompoly*] that used to be on the cartridge pouches were also discontinued. Along with this, a new pattern of **bandolier**, or shoulder belt, [*pantaler ili pogonnaya perevyaz'*] was confirmed for Carabiniers, with brass fittings, iron hook, and ramrod strap [162].

13 April 1835 – When in or out of formation, officers were ordered to use a toggle to fasten one end of the **shako line** to a loop fashioned at the back of the shako from the shako cord, as laid out above for the previous regiment [163].

19 July 1835 - To stow the pistol, it was ordered to have a **holder** [*chushka*] on the left side of the swordbelt [*portupeya*], on the same basis as set forth above for Army Dragoon regiments. Beginning in this same year **pelisses** began to be worn over the back instead of on the left shoulder (Illus. 746) [164].

31 January 1836 – In the L.-Gds. Hussar Regiment, lower ranks' **greatcoats** were to have nine buttons, as in the L.-Gds. Horse-Grenadiers; in the L.-Gds. Grodno Hussars, these greatcoats were to have 11 buttons, as in the L.-Gds. Dragoon Regiment [165].

13 May 1836 - Officers' **saddle girths** [*podprugi*] were to be dark green with red stripes [166].

9 October 1836 – As a place for their pistols, staff-trumpeters and trumpeters were to have **holders** [*chushki*] of a special pattern that could be fitted to the saddle over the saddle cloth on the left side. For cartridges they were to have **cartridge pouches** [*lyadunki*] with crossbelts, as for other lower ranks (Illus. 747) [167].

14 February 1837 - Staff-trumpeters and trumpeters, who in mounted formation are prescribed pistols and—for cartridges—pouches and crossbelts, were ordered to also wear these **cartridge pouches** when in dismounted formation [168].

11 March 1837 - The muskets [*ruzh'ya*] in both regiments were replaced with short **carbines** [*karabiny*] of the same pattern as those introduced in other Hussar regiments [169].

17 December 1837 - A new pattern of officers' **epaulettes** (for the undress coat) was confirmed, identical with that introduced at this time in the regiments, i.e. with an additional, fourth, row of braid [170].

23 February 1838 - Regulations were confirmed concerning the saddle's **pistol holders** [*pistoletnyya chushki*] mandated on 9 October 1836, as set forth above (see the preceding cavalry regiments) [171].

21 May 1838 - New patterns were confirmed for the **pelisse** [*mentik*] and **dolman**. The pelisse was ordered to be made so that it could be worn over the dolman with the sleeves hanging loose [*v rukava*] (Illus. 748) [172].

4 January 1839 - The **riding-trousers** [*reituzy*] of generals and field and company-grade officers were not to have any bows or bands in front [*speredi bantov ne imet'*] but rather worn completely smooth [*gladkii*] in the manner prescribed for lower ranks [173].

16 October 1840 - A regulation concerning lower ranks' gold and silver **chevrons** [*shevrony*] was confirmed (see Grenadier regiments) [174].

23 January 1841 - The capes [*bolshie vorotniki*] of officers' **greatcoats** were to be 1 arshin [28 inches] long as measured from the bottom edge of the collar [*malyi vorotnik*] [175].

8 April 1843 - Officers and combatant lower ranks were given a new pattern **shako** [*kiver*] 4-3/4 vershoks [8 1/4 inches] high and curving inward a little toward the bottom (Illus. 749). Along with this, in order to distinguish rank among the lower ranks, it was ordered to have **shoulder cords** [*epoletnye snurki*] with small slides [*gombochki*] on both shoulders of the pelisse as well as the dolman. **Greatcoat shoulder straps** were to have sewn-on galloon and tape according to the scheme laid out for Army Hussar regiments [176].

10 May 1843 - Cover flaps [*kryshki*] for **cartridge pouches** [*lyadunki*] were to be (with the cover sewn to the box): 4-1/2 vershoks [8 inches] long, 4-7/8 vershoks [9 inches] wide at the top edge, and 5-5/8 vershoks [10 inches] wide along the bottom edge. The oval belt rings for **carbines** are to be replaced with circular ones. Belts were attached to the stocks of the carbines by means of special straps with buckles, and in order to avoid the upper brass band hitting the spurs, as well as so that the carbines did not drag on the ground when dismounted, they were to be raised up by shortening the bandolier, according to the height of the individual [177].

2 January 1844 - Officers were to have a **cockade** on the band of the forage cap, as indicated above (see the preceding forces) (Illus. 750) [178].

19 February 1844 - The shortening of the **bandolier** according to the height of the soldier, as laid down on 10 May 1843, was ordered to be done using the brass buckle at its end so that its lower end was even with the lower edge of the dolman. [179].

1844 May 20 - A new scheme for the different **forage caps** of lower ranks was confirmed, based on which they were confirmed to be the same color as the dolman, with piping around the top edge to be: in a regiment's 1st double-squadron [*divizion*] — red, in the 2nd — white, in the 3rd — light blue [*svetlosinii*], and in the reserve [*rezervnyi*] and replacement [*zapasnyi*] squadrons — dark green. The cap band was prescribed to be the same color as the shako, with piping around the edges according to the color of the buttons: of yellow cloth for brass buttons and white for tin. The band also had the cut-out number of the squadron and the Cyrillic letter "Е" [for *eskadron* — M.C]. For officers the cap band was the same as for lower ranks and with the same piping, but without numerals or letters, while the piping around the top of the forage cap was the same color as the piping on the band [180].

21 September 1844 - **Non-commissioned officer standard-bearers** [*shtandartnye unter-ofitsery*] in formation were ordered to always have the cartridge pouch under the crossbelt for the standard [181].

17 December 1844 - In order to distinguish **rank** between generals and field and company-grade officers, dolmans and pelisses were to have cords and slides [*snurki i gombochki*] with small stars: silver plated in the L.-Gds. Hussar Regiment and gilt in the L.-Gds. Grodno Hussars, and in the same number as how many of stars were on the epaulettes (Illus. 351) [182].

27 January 1845 – Instead of shakos, all combatant ranks in the Guards Hussar regiments were given **bearskin headdresses** with the previous chinscales and—in the L.-Gds. Hussars—a red cloth bag, and in the L.-Gds. Grodno Hussars—a light-blue one. The bags were trimmed with tape for lower ranks and with galloon for officers, of the same color as the uniform braid. Plumes on the headdresses were to be of horse hair: red for trumpeters and white for other ranks (Illus. 751 and 752) [183].

26 February 1845 - Instead of undress coats [*vitse-mundiry*], field and company-grade officers of both regiments were ordered to have **jackets** [*kurtki*] (very dark blue in the L.-Gds. Hussar Regiment and light blue in the L.-Gds. Grodno Hussars trimmed with gold or silver cord [*snurki*], as well as galloon for field-grade officers, according to the color of the cord and galloon on pelisses and dolmans. **Riding trousers** worn with these jackets were kept the same as before, of blue-grey cloth (Illus. 753). Generals in hussar uniforms were also allowed to wear such jackets in place of the undress coat [184].

14 April 1845 – For **generals** entitled to wear the uniform of the L.-Gds. Hussars or L.-Gds. Grodno Hussars, a **feather** [*pero*] in place of a plume was established for the fur headdress, after the pattern prescribed for cossack generals [185].

18 August 1845 - With the newly introduced jackets, officers with troop units [*vo fronte*] were ordered to have the **sabertache** in a cover [*chekhol*], and instead of frock coats [*syurtuki*] they were given new-pattern **vengerki** coats [literally, "Hungarians" - M.C.] of the same colors as the jacket (Illus. 754). Generals were allowed to wear the previous undress coats and frocks [186].

8 September 1845 - With the **jacket** introduced on 26 February 1845, officers on duty and holding official positions [*na dezhurstvakh i v dolzhnostyakh*] were ordered to wear the cartridge pouch, girdle, and sabertache in case [187].

15 November 1845 - Both regiments were ordered to have **pioneer axes** [*shantsovye topory*], two in each platoon, plus 56 iron **shovels** [*lopaty*] in each regiment, as noted above (see the preceding Guards cavalry regiments) [188].

7 August 1846 – This date's confirmed descriptions of fitting firing-cap pouches [*kapsyul'nye sumochki*] and stowing the tin case [*zhestyanoi futlyar*], small valise [*chemodanchik*], and piston screwdriver [*pistonnaya otverka*], set forth in detail in the chapter for Guards Dragoon regiments, were also applied to Hussar regiments with the difference that their **firing-cap pouches** were fitted to the crossbelt not on the right side of the chest, but the left, 1-1/2 vershoks [2-5/8 inches] below the shoulder cords [*epoletnyi shurok*] [189].

13 September 1846 – New pattern carriers [*kobury*] were approved for officers' percussion lock **pistols** (see Army Cuirassier regiments) [190].

26 October 1846 - The collars on **generals' uniform coats** [*mundiry*] were ordered to be open [*razreznyi*] (Illus. 755) [191].

19 May 1847 - **Forage caps** were established for lower noncombatant ranks, the same as in Guards infantry regiments [192].

9 January 1848 - Field and company-grade officers, on those days when holiday uniform [*prazdnichnaya forma*] was prescribed after guard mount [*posle razvoda*], were allowed to wear, for walking out [*dlya progulok*], **vengerki** coats with riding trousers and headdresses with plumes [193].

19 January 1848 – Confirmation was given to a description of the **firing-cap pouch** [*kapsyulnaya sumochka*] worn with the officer's cartridge pouch (see Army Cuirassier regiments) [194].

25 April 1848 - The **valise's flap** [*klapan na chemodane*] with buttons was completely done away with [195].

17 December 1849 - **Greatcoats** for officers and lower ranks were to have a collar the same color as the dolman, with yellow or white piping around the collar according to the color of the appointment. Shoulder straps for lower ranks were to be the same color as the bag on the headdress (Illus. 756) [196].

24 December 1849 - The grips of the **gold swords** awarded for bravery were directed to be gold [197].

5 March 1850 - **Bandoliers** for standards were ordered to be 2-1/2 vershoks [4-3/8 inches] wide, 2 arshins [4-1/2] feet long, and lined on the outside in the L.-Gds. Hussar Regiment with very dark-blue velvet with gold trim, and in the L.-Gds. Grodno Hussars with light-blue velvet with silver trim. In both regiments the inner side was to be lined with red cloth [198].

3 February 1851 – Covers were established for lower ranks' **headdresses**, capable of having the chinscales tied over them in the manner for officers, with a read piece that folded up into the interior [199].

30 March 1851 - Approval was given to descriptions of **cartridge-pouch belts**, **bandoliers**, and **firing-cap pouches** (see Army Cuirassier regiments) [200].

3 January 1852 - Cases or coverings [*chekhly, ili nakladki*] for the **firing nipples** [*sterzhni*] of percussion weapons were introduced, as established for Army Infantry on 8 July 1851 [201].

26 January 1852 – The band on noncombatants' gray **forage caps** was directed to be the same color as the collars of combatant lower ranks [202].

12 July 1852 - In order to achieve uniformity in dress, officers were ordered to have red **jackets** instead of the previous ones, to be worn at all those times when the dark-blue jackets were previously prescribed. Additionally, they were to wear them when in camp uniform and with troop units [*pri lagernoi forme i vo fronte*], when lower ranks were in dolmans, i.e. in summer campaign dress (Illus. 757) [203].

16 July 1852 - Cases or coverings for **firing nipples** were established in accordance with the description confirmed for Cuirassier regiments [204].

29 August 1852 - In order to be distinguished from company-grade officers, field-grade officers were ordered to have galloon on the collars of their **vengerki** and **jackets**, this galloon being of the newly confirmed pattern, similar to the galloon prescribed for their sleeves (Illus. 757) [205].

3 January 1853 - Non-combatant lower ranks in the L.-Gds. Grodno Hussar Regiment were ordered to have bands and piping on their **forage caps** of the same colors as prescribed for combantant lower ranks' caps [206].

13 August 1853 - Generals and field and company-grade officers, when in the campaign uniform [*pokhodnaya forma*] of a *vengerka* coat without girdle, were directed to buckle the **swordbelt** [*portupeya*] over the *vengerka* [207].

15 November 1853 – Confirmation was given to a description for rolling **greatcoats** on saddles, a description of officers' **horse furniture**, the list of **items** which a soldier was to have at inspections, and a description of sundry articles and the directions on where to stow them (see Army Cuirassier regiments) [208].

18 February 1854 - The regulation of 15 November 1853 concerning light-cavalry **horse furniture**, presented above in the section for Army Cuirassier regiments, was also extended to Guards Hussar regiments [209].

29 April 1854 - During wartime, generals and field and company-grade officers were to have **campaign greatcoats** [*pokhodnyya shineli*] of the same color and pattern as the greatcoats of lower ranks. With these greatcoats it was prescribed to wear swordbelts and pouchbelts; girdles were not to worn (Illus. 758) [210].

XLI. LIFE-GUARDS GENDARME HALF-SQUADRON. [*Leib-Gvardii Zhandarmskiipolueskadron.*].

12 April 1826 – All combatant ranks, instead of their white pants and high boots, were given lancer-pattern *chakchiry* **pants** of light-blue [*svetlosinii*] cloth, the same color as the coat, with piping on the side seams and wide red stripes. For lower ranks the pants also had leather reinforcement at the bottom (Illus. 759). The same wide stripes were also established for the riding trousers, in place of the previous light-blue [211].

15 September 1826 – For lower ranks who served out the regulation number of years without reproach and who voluntarily remained on service there was established **gold galloon** to be worn on the left sleeve, as described above for grenadier regiments [212].

30 December 1826 – **Broadswords** [*palashi*] were issued in place of sabers [*sabli*], identical to those introduced on 8 October 1827 for all Guards and Army cavalry regiments (Illus. 759) [213].

1 January 1827 - Small forged and stamped stars on officers' epaulettes were established to distinguish **rank**, in the same scheme as set forth above for Army Cuirassiers regiments [214].

9 May 1827 – All combatant ranks were given new pattern **helmets** with hanging plumes, wider and longer than before, with the previous fittings. These helmets were identical to those confirmed at this same time for Army Cuirassier regiments (Illus. 760) [215].

19 June 1827 – Officers were ordered to wear **frock coats** and **greatcoats** of light-blue [*svetlosinii*] cloth the same color as the dress coat, with red piping and likewise red tabs on the greatcoat collar (Illus. 761) [216].

14 December 1827 - The lace [*nashivka*] sewn onto lower ranks' left sleeves as instituted on 15 September 1826 was ordered to be silver non-commissioned officers' galloon [217].

24 March 1828 - Lower ranks were forbidden to have cinches [*peretyazhki*] on their **coats** [218].

9 July 1829 - The wide stripes [*lampasy*] on officers' and lower ranks' **riding trousers** [*reituzy*] were removed, and only piping was left on the side seams [219].

26 December 1829 - All combatant ranks were ordered to have uniform **buttons** with the raised image of a two-headed eagle [220].

8 June 1832 – Officers were allowed to wear **moustaches** [221].

15 April 1834 – New pattern **cartridge pouches** and **crossbelts** were established, with smaller lids and a narrower belt [222].

2 May 1834 - In order to improve handling of the **saber**, its hilt was ordered to be remade according to a new pattern, as in Army Dragoon regiments [223].

4 February 1835 – New pattern **helmets** were confirmed, lower than before and identical with those introduced in Army Cuirassier regiments [224].

28 February 1835 – Both mounted and dismounted non-commissioned officers and privates were prescribed one **pistol** each [225].

27 March 1835 - Lower ranks in dismounted order were directed to carry the **musket** in the right hand following the example of the L.-Gds. Horse-Grenadier Regiment (Illus. 762), and when in mounted formation—in the bucket [*bushmat*] as previously [226].

11 August 1835 – Following the example of the privates, non-commissioned officers were given **muskets** [227].

31 January 1836 – Instead of 12 buttons, 11 were prescribed for lower ranks' **greatcoats**, a laid out above for Army Cuirassier regiments [228].

9 October 1836 - As a place for their pistols, trumpeters were to have special pattern **holders** [*chushki*], fitted to the saddle over the saddlecloth on the left. For cartridges they were to have **cartridge pouches** [*lyadunki*] with crossbelts, as for other lower ranks [229].

17 January 1837 – Confirmation was given to rules on how officers were to wear the **saber with the frock coat**, as set forth above for Grenadier and Lancer regiments [230].

14 February 1837 - Trumpeters who were prescribed pistols when in mounted formation and—for cartridges—pouches with belts, were ordered to also wear these **cartridge pouches** when in dismounted formation [231].

15 July 1837 - A new pattern of officers' **sash** was confirmed, identical with that described above for Grenadier regiments [232].

17 December 1837 – A new style of officers' **epaulette** was confirmed, identical to that introduced for preceding troops, i.e. with an additional, fourth, twist of narrow braid [233].

11 January 1838 - Approval was given to a description of the officer's **saddle** designated for use on 6 March 1834, in agreement in all details with that presented above for Army Dragoon regiments [234].

23 February 1838 - Regulations were confirmed concerning the **pistol holders** [*pistoletnyya chushki*] introduced for the saddle on 9 October 1836, described in detail above for Army Dragoon regiments [235].

4 January 1839 - The *chakchiry* **pants and riding trousers** of officers were ordered to not have any bows or bands in front [*speredi bantov ne imet*] but rather worn completely smooth [*gladkii*], as established for lower ranks [236].

16 October 1840 - A regulation concerning silver **chevrons** [*shevrony*] for lower ranks was confirmed, as set forth in detail above for Grenadier regiments [237].

23 January 1841 - The capes [*bolshie vorotniki*] of officers' **greatcoats** were to be 1 arshin [28 inches] long as measured from the bottom edge of the collar [*maly vorotnik*] [238].

8 April 1843 – All combatant ranks were ordered to not have knots on their **aiguillettes** between the loops and the metal ends. The previous woolen tassels on lower ranks' sword knots were replaced by leather ones, after the example of light cavalry regiments [239]. On this same date, in order to distinguish **rank** among the lower ranks, lace [*nashivki*] was established to be sewn onto epaulettes and shoulder straps in accordance with the scheme prescribed for the Gendarme Regiment, but with the army tape replaced by guards pattern [240].

10 May 1843 - Cover flaps [*kryshki*] for **cartridge pouches**, sewn to the box, were to be 4-1/2 vershoks [8 inches] long, 4-7/8 vershoks [9 inches] wide at the top edge, and 5-5/8 vershoks [10 inches] wide along the bottom edge [241].

2 January 1844 – A cockade was instituted for the band on officers' **forage caps**, as related above for grenadier regiments [242].

27 April 1845 – The previous **helmets** with high plumes were replaced by new ones with a hanging plume, of red horse hair for trumpeters and white for other ranks. The helmet was of the pattern introduced for Guards Cuirassier regiments, and the badge on it was left as before (Illus. 763). For these same helmets, instead of grenades with the plumes, it was ordered that there be silver two-headed eagles, to be fitted at such times as would be directed (Illus. 764) [243].

7 August 1846 – A description of how to fit **firing-cap pouches** was confirmed (see Dragoon regiments) [244].

13 September 1846 – New carriers [*kobury*] were approved for officers' percussion **pistols** [245].

9 January 1848 - Field and company-grade officers, on those days when after guard mount [*posle razvoda*] they had to remain in holiday uniform [*prazdnichnaya forma*], were allowed to wear, for walking out [*dlya progulok*], **frock coats** with *chakchiry* pants, along with **helmets** with plumes [246].

25 April 1848 - The **valise**'s flap with buttons was removed [247].

24 December 1849- The grips of **gold swords** awarded for bravery were prescribed to be gold [248].

30 March 1851 – **Cartridge-pouch belts** were prescribed to be 1 vershok (1-3/4 inches) wide and carry the previous firing-cap pouch [249].

13 August 1853 – Field and company-grade officers, when in campaign uniform and wearing **frock coats** without the sash, were ordered to wear the sword belt over the frock [250].

15 November 1853 – Confirmation was given to descriptions of rolling soldiers' **greatcoats**, officers' **horse furniture**, and the sundry **items** needed by a cavalry soldier (see Army Cuirassier regiments) [251].

18 February 1854 – The directives laid down regarding **light-cavalry horse furniture** on 15 November 1853 were also extended to the L.-Gds. Gendarme Half-Squadron [252].

29 April 1854- During wartime, generals and field and company-grade officers were to have **campaign greatcoats** of the same color and cut as for soldiers [253].

XLII. GUARDS TRAIN. [*Gvardeiskii furshtat.*]

15 September 1826 - For lower ranks who served out the regulation number of years without reproach and who voluntarily remained on service there was established **gold galloon** to be worn on the left sleeve, as described above for grenadier regiments [254].

1 January 1827 - Small forged and stamped stars on officers' epaulettes were established to distinguish **rank**, as set forth in detail above for grenadier regiments [255].

8 October 1827 - New pattern **sabers** were established for lower ranks, with a brass hilt, black grip, and iron scabbard, straighter than before, as described above for Army Dragoon regiments (Illus. 765) [256].

13 October 1827 – Officers were given **epaulettes** with scaled fields, of the pattern introduced to the cavalry forces above (Illus. 766). Along with this **shoulder straps** were established for lower ranks: red in the 1st Battalion, light blue [*svetlosinii*] in the 2nd, white in the 3rd, green piped red in the 4th, and for the Guards Train quartered in Warsaw—dark blue with red piping [257].

14 December 1827 - The **lace** [*nashivka*] sewn onto lower ranks' left sleeves, instituted on 15 September 1826, was ordered to be silver [258].

24 April 1828 – Lower ranks' **coats** were forbidden to have cinches [259].

17 February 1829 – New pattern **shakos** and **plates** were established for the Guards Train, the same as prescribed for troops of the Guards Corps, but for lower ranks without cords (Illus. 766). Cavalry **galloon** was established for non-commissioned officers, and officers were to wear **moustaches** [260].

9 July 1829 – Apart from the *chakchiry* pants with wide stripes, for the Guards Train there were also established **riding trousers** with light-blue piping in the side seams [261].

8 October 1829 – Dark-blue shako **pompons** were established for lower ranks in Guards Train battalions (Illus. 767) [262].

26 December 1829 - All combatant ranks of the Guards Train were ordered to have uniform **buttons** with the raised image of a two-headed eagle, as prescribed for the shako plate [263].

4 April 1830 – Silver **pompons** were established for officers' shakos [264].

28 August 1830 – For lower ranks in the Guards Train there were established **shoulder straps** the same color as the band on the forage cap of the regiment to which they assigned, i.e. in the L.-Gds. Preobrazhenskii and Moscow Regiments—red; the Semenovskii and Grenadiers—light blue; the Izmailovskii and Pavlovsk—white with red piping; the Jägers and Finland—dark green with red piping; in the Guards Trains stationed in Warsaw—yellow [265].

21 April 1831 – The Train assigned to the Guards troops stationed in **Warsaw** was prescribed the same uniforms as the rest of the Guards Train, i.e. without raspberry piping, and with the image of St. George the Bearer of Victory in the eagle's shield, on the buttons, and on the shako plate [266].

13 October 1831 – For the newly established Train with the **L.-Gds. Horse-Pioneer Squadron** the same uniform as prescribed as for the rest of the Guards Train, with red shoulder straps and shako plates and buttons as for the squadron's combatant ranks [267].

4 December 1832 – Guards Train personnel with heavy and light cavalry regiments were prescribed to have red tabs on coat and greatcoat **collars**, black tabs when with artillery, and black with red piping when with sappers and pioneers [268].

1 February 1833 – With a new listing of the different **shoulder-strap** colors for lower rank Train personnel with all the Guards regiments, these were prescribed to be:

In the Preobrazhenskii Regiment—red with white piping.
In the Semenovskii—light blue with white piping.
In the Izmailovskii—white with red piping.
In the Jägers—green with white piping.
In the Moscow—red.
In the Grenadiers—light blue.
In the Pavlovsk—white.
In the Finland—green with red piping.
In the Guards Équipage—white with green piping.
In the Lithuania—red with yellow piping.
In the Emperor of Austria's Grenadiers—light blue with yellow piping.
In the King of Prussia's Grenadiers—white with yellow piping.
In the Volhynia—green with yellow piping.
In all these regiments, the collars on coats and greatcoats were to light blue.

Shoulder straps in Her Majesty's Cavalier Guards—red with white piping.
In the L.-Gds. Horse—white with red piping.
In His Majesty's Cuirassiers—white with light blue piping.
In the Heir and Tsesarevich's Leib-Cuirassiers—white with raspberry piping.
In the Horse-Grenadiers—red with green piping.
In the Lancers—dark blue with red pipng.
In the Hussars—red with dark blue piping.]
In the Dragoons—green with red piping.
In Her Imperial Highness Grand Duke Michael Pavlovich's Lancers—dark blue with yellow piping.
In the Grodno Hussars—green with raspberry piping.
In all these regiments the collars of coats and greatcoats were to have red tabs with white buttons.

Shoulder straps in the L.-Gds. 1st Artillery Brigade--black with white piping.
In the L.-Gds. 2nd Artillery Brigade—black with red piping.
In the 3rd Guards and Grenadier Artillery Brigade—black with yellow piping.
In the L.-Gds. Sapper Battalion—black.
The tabs on the collars of coats and greatcoats were black with white buttons.
Shoulder straps in the Guards Horse Artillery—black with red piping; tabs on collars were also black, with red piping and white buttons.
Shoulder straps in the L.-Gds. Horse-Pioneer Squadron—black; tabs were also black, with white buttons [269].
2 May 1834 - In order to improve handling of the **saber**, its hilt was ordered to be remade according to a new pattern, as set forth above for Army Dragoon regiments [270].
7 December 1834 - **Shako cords** on officers' shakos, when these shakos were being worn, were ordered to no longer reach to the waist, but only halfway down the back [271].
5 February 1835 – Instead of white **shoulder straps** piped with raspberry, lower rank Train personnel with the Heir and Tsesarevich's Leib-Cuirassier Regiment were prescribed light blue piped white [272].
13 April 1835 - When in formation, officers of the L.-Gds. Dragoon Regiment were ordered to use a toggle to fasten one end of the **shako cord** to a loop made behind the shako using the cord itself, and at all other times, when obliged to take off the shako, this cord was to be detached from the loop, whereupon it was left around the neck with its slide, which was to be in back at the middle of the neck, and the end with the toggle was to be fastened to the second coat button from the top so that the cord passed under the right arm [273].
31 January 1836 – Nine buttons were prescribed for lower ranks' **greatcoats** instead of ten [274].
27 April 1836 - **Pompons** were ordered to be backed with black leather [275].
17 January 1837 – Rules were confirmed regarding how officers were to wear **sabers** with the frock coat, as set forth above for Guards Lancer regiments [276].
15 July 1837 - A new pattern of officers' **sash** was confirmed, identical to that described above for Grenadier regiments [277].
17 December 1837 – A new patter of officers' **epaulette** was confirmed, identical to that described above for preceding troops, i.e. with the addition of a fourth twist of braid [278].
11 January 1838 - Approval was given to a description of the officer's **saddle**, in agreement in all details with that presented above for Army Dragoon regiments [279].
4 January 1839 - The **pants** of generals and field and company-grade officers were not to have any bows or bands in front but rather worn completely plain, in the same manner as established for lower ranks [280].
13 July 1839 – Train officers with the L.-Gds. Sapper Battalion were prescribed scaled **epaulettes**, after the example of other Train officers [281].
16 October 1840 - The regulation concerning lower ranks' **chevrons** [shevrony] was confirmed, as set forth above for Grenadier regiments [282].
29 October 1840 – The sapper armature of two axes was established for **buttons** and **shako plates** of Train personnel with the L.-Gds. Sapper Battalion [283].
23 January 1841 - The capes of officers' **greatcoats** were to be 1 arshin [28 inches] long as measured from the bottom edge of the collar [284].
8 April 1843 – For lower ranks in the Guards Train there were established sword knots with leather tassels instead of the previous woolen ones. On this same date, in order to distinguish **rank** among the lower ranks, lace [nashivki] was established to be sewn onto shoulder straps following the same scheme as described above for Grenadier regiments, except with gold galloon replaced by silver and white tape by yellow. Also confirmed were new pattern shakos identical to those established for Grenadiers, Infantry, and other regiments, i.e. lower than previously and slighty tapered towards the bottom (Illus. 768) [285].
2 January 1844 - Officers were to have a **cockade** on the band of the forage cap, as set forth above for preceding troops [286].
12 April 1844 – For lower rank Train personnel with the His Majesty's L.-Gds. Cuirassiers and His Highness the Heir and Tsesarevich's Leib-Cuirassiers **shoulder straps** were ordered to be: light blue piped white for the first, and white with light-blue piping for the second [287].
9 May 1844 – The Guards Train was given **helmets** [kaski] in place of shakos, identical to those introduced for other troops, without plumes and with the same plates as were on the shakos (Illus. 769) [288].
20 May 1844 – **Forage caps** were established for lower ranks Guards Train personnel, colored gray with a light-blue band

on which were to be cut out, in yellow cloth, the company number and Cyrillic letter R, with light-blue piping around the crown. Officers were to have dark-green forage caps with light-blue bands and piping, and as before—without numbers or letters [289].

23 September 1844 – All non-commissioned officers in the Guards Train were prescribed **saddles** without saddlecloths, of the artillery pattern [290].

4 January 1845 - Officers' **helmets** were to have a cockade on the right side under the chin-scales (Illus. 770) [291].

19 May 1847 - Lower non-combatant ranks were prescribed gray **forage caps** with light-blue bands without cutout letters or numbers, and with light-blue piping around the top [292].

9 January 1848 - Generals, and field and company-grade officers, on those days when after guard mount they had to remain in holiday uniform, were allowed to wear, for walking out, **frock coats** with *chakchiry* pants, along with **helmets** [293].

25 April 1848 - The **valise's** flap with buttons was removed [294].

17 April 1852 – The remaking of **water flasks**, and the method of fitting them, as laid down on 8 July 1851, were extended to the Train, with the only difference being that the flask was to worn over the shoulder and the strap have a buckle added in order to make adjustments according to the size of the individual and the order of dress being worn [295].

13 August 1853 – Company-grade officers, when in campaign dress of **frock coats** without sashes, were ordered to wear the sword belt on the outside of the frock coat [296].

18 February 1854 – The regulations laid down on 15 November 1853 regarding light-cavalry **horse furniture** were extended to the Train [297].

29 April 1854 - Company-grade officers in wartime were ordered to have **campaign greatcoats** of the same cut and color as soldiers' greatcoats [298].

XLIII. GUARDS FOOT ARTILLERY. [*Gvardeiskaya peshaya artilleriya.*]

11 September 1826 – For company-grade officers of Guards Foot Artillery, instead of gray riding trousers and dark-green pants with high boots, and lower combatant ranks, instead of dark-green pants with knee gaiters—there were established long dark-green pants of the pattern introduced for Guards Infantry, with red piping in the side seams. Lower ranks at all times, and company-grade officers only when in formation or anytime when wearing sashes, were to wear black cloth **half-gaiters** [*polushtiblety*] under these pants and over the boots, fastened with five or six small metal buttons the same color as the coat buttons (Illus. 771 and 772). Generals, field-grade officers, and adjutants were to have the same pants as combatants but were ordered to not have gaiters, but rather wear boots with the **spurs** driven in. Along with this change, the horizontal belt for the **knapsack** was ordered to be above the lower buttons of the coat, while the **greatcoat** was to be carried on the knapsack rolled into a tube in its special oilskin case made of raven's-duck (Illus. 772). Clerks and in general all non-combatant lower ranks were prescribed gray riding trousers without wide stripes [299].

10 May 1826 - Generals, field-grade officers, and those company-grade officers who were by regulation mounted when in formation, were ordered during the summer to wear white linen **pants** [*polotnyanyya pantalony*] without integral spats [*kozyrki*], of the same pattern as previously described for the dark-green ones (Illus. 773). In addition, suede [*zamshevyya*] pants of the same pattern were permitted to be worn instead of the linen pants [200].

15 September 1826 - Lower ranks who had completed the regulation number of years of faultless service and had the right to be discharged but who voluntarily remained on active duty were to wear a **gold galloon** stripe sewn onto the left sleeve in addition to the yellow tape established on 29 March 1825 [301].

12 December 1826 – Officers' épées [*shpagi*] were replaced by **half-sabers** [*polusabli*] of the same pattern as introduced on 20 August 1830 for Army infantry and described above for Grenadier regiments [302].

1 January 1827 - Officers' **epaulettes** were to have small forged and stamped silver stars as rank distinctions, and of the same pattern and scheme as set forth above for preceding troops [303].

14 February 1827 – **Cuff flaps** in the 2nd Guards Artillery Brigade, instead of being dark green with red piping, were ordered to be red with dark-green piping (Illus. 774). Pocket flaps on officers' coats in the Guards Foot Artillery were prescribed to be without red piping [304].

23 March 1827 - Mounted helpers [*gandlangery*, from German *Handlanger* — M.C.] were ordered to wear **riding trousers** [*reituzy*] with wide stripes when mounted, and dark-green **trousers** [*bryuki*] with gaiters [*shtiblety*] when on foot. In summer they were to wear **summer pants** [*letniya pantalony*] [305].

31 July 1827 - Numbers and letters on the **covers** for shakos and pouches were ordered changed from yellow cloth to yellow oil paint [306].

19 November 1827 – It was ordered that there be red cloth piping on the lower edge of the **collar** of coats and greatcoats [307].

24 March 1828 - The **coats** of lower ranks were forbidden to have cinches [308].

24 April 1828 – The following changed in uniform clothing and accouterments were introduced:

1. New pattern **shakos** were prescribed: 5-1/2 vershoks [9-5/8 inches] high, with an upper diameter not less than 5-5/8 vershoks [9-7/8 inches] and not more than 6 [10-1/2], the lower diameter being according to the size of the head. The width of upper lacquered edge was 5/16 vershoks [9/16 inches] (Illus. 775 and 776).

2. The **shako plate**, in connection with the shako's greater size, was prescribed to be of a new pattern: in the 1st and 2nd Brigades with an image of St. George the Bearer of Victory in the eagle's shield, but in Battery No. 5 Company with an image of a Lithuanian horseman in the shield.

3. **Shako cords** were also to be of a new pattern, of red cord, around the top of the shako and with small tassels and bows hanging from the right side, even with the shako's lower edge. For canoneers and bombardiers the cords were all red, for fireworkers—white with black and orange. Cords, tassels, and bows were silver for officers.

4. The width of the **crossbelt** and **swordbelt** was stipulated as 2 vershoks [3-1/2 inches], of the **knapsack shoulder belts**—1-1/2 vershoks [2-5/8 inches], and of the **belt across the chest** [*nagrudnyi remen*]—1-1/8 vershoks [2 inches].

5. **Knapsacks** [*rantsy*] were to be of calfskin as before but with black leather trim. The knapsack was prescribed to be 9 vershoks [15-3/4 inches] by 2-1/2 [4-3/8 inches] in breadth and depth, and 8 vershoks [14 inches] high. The length of the cover from the upper edge was 6 vershoks [10-1/2 inches].

6. In place of their grey coats [*mundiry*], all non-combatant non-commissioned officers were to be issued dark-green **frock coats** [*syurtuki*] with a single row of buttons and the same collar, cuffs, and shoulder straps as for combatant personnel. **Pants** were grey with red piping on the side seams.

7. Non-combatant lower rank craftsmen [*masterovye*], as well as medical orderlies [*lazaretnye sluzhiteli*] were to replace their coats with grey cloth **jackets** [*kurtki*] modeled on the coat. **Pants** were to be as for the non-combatants above [309].

18 May 1829 - Non-commissioned officers who had been recommended by higher command for promotion to officer rank by virtue of years of service were permitted to have **silver sword-knots** [310].

8 October 1829 - Mounted helpers [*gandlangery*] were prescribed **riding trousers** without wide stripes, having only red piping on the side seams [311].

16 December 1829 – The black cuffs on officers' **frock coats** were changed to dark green, with red piping as before [312].

26 December 1829 – For all ranks the **buttons** on dress coats, frock coats, and greatcoats were prescribed to have are raised image of the two-headed eagle as found on the shako plate [313].

19 June 1831 – For the L.-Gds. Battery No. 5 Company the eagle's shield on **buttons** and **shako plate** was to have, instead of a Lithuanian horseman, an depiction of St. George the Bearer of Victory. The greatcoat collar was to have black cloth tabs with red piping, with the buttons prescribed for the dress coat [314].

1 January 1832 - Generals who have the gold swords with diamonds inscribed "*za khrabost*" ["*for courage*"] were ordered not to use **sword-knots** [315].

8 June 1832 – Generals and field and company-grade officers were permitted to wear **moustaches** [316].

3 January 1833 - **Cloth half-gaiters** were abolished for company-grade officers and lower ranks (Illus. 777). **Swordknots** were abolished for non-commissioned officers and privates except for those non-commissioned officers who had them in silver [317].

20 February 1833 - All combatant ranks were given new pattern **summer pants or trousers** [*letniya pantalony ili bryuki*], without buttons or integral spats (Illus. 778) [318].

16 April 1833 – Field and company-grade officers who had to be mounted when in formation were permitted to have **horses** with long tails [319].

28 December 1833 – With the general reorganization of the entire Guards artillery and the renaming of the 6th Infantry Corps' Combined-Guards and Grenadier Artillery Brigades as the 3rd Guards and Grenadier Artillery Brigade, their previous **uniforms** were retained, i.e. in the L.-Gds. 5th Battery Battery the same uniform as the 1st and 2nd Guards Brigades; in the 6th Battery Battery—with gold buttonhole loops on the collar and cuff flaps of officer's dress coats; in 3rd Light Battery—without buttonhole loops (Illus. 779 and 780). Along with this the **horses** in all three brigades were ordered to be of the same color in each battery, i.e. in the 1st, 3rd, and 5th Battery Batteries—sorrels, in the 2nd, 4th, and 6th—blacks, and in the 1st, 2nd, and 3rd Light Batteries—bays. All **officers** when in formation were to always be mounted and wearing spurs [320].

28 March 1834 - Highest Authority confirmed a new pattern for **short-swords** [*tesaki*] with a straight blade (Illus. 781) [321].

26 April 1834 - **Numbers** and **letters** on shako covers and travel caps [*dorozhnyya shapki*] were to be as follows: in the 1st battery company—Cyrillic *1.B.*, in the 1st light company—Cyrillic *1.L.*, and so on. The upper piping on forage caps [*furazhnyya shapki*] in the first battery batteries was prescribed to be red, in the second—white, in the third—light blue, and in reserve companies—yellow. In all of these companies the upper and lower piping of the cap band was prescribed to be red, with yellow numbers and letters on the band (322).

14 May 1834 - An new pattern **saddle** for Guards artillery officers was confirmed, of black leather. For parades shabracks were left as before, with gold galloon and stars. For everyday use there were everyday shabracks without stars, of the same pattern as parade shabracks but with the gold galloon changed to black velvet stripes, with red piping along both sides of the stripes. Surcingles for these shabracks were prescribed to be of black and red stripes. The same saddles and shabracks, completely similar to the undress shabracks [*vits-chepraki*] of Guards artillery companies, were also established for everyday use in Grenadier companies of the 3rd Guards and Grenadier Artillery Brigade (323).

29 May 1834 – It was ordered that under no circumstances were officers to wear **knapsacks** when in formation. At all times they were to wear **spurs** and have straps [*podmochki*] on the pants to pass under the sole of the boot (324).

26 September 1834 - Lower ranks were directed to wear the **knapsack** on two belts lying crosswise over the chest (Illus. 782)(325).

20 August 1835 - It was ordered that for lower ranks a linen case or pocket [*kholshchevyi chekhol ili karman*] for the forage cap was to be put on the outside of **knapsack** on the side that lay on the soldier's back. These cases were to be made from the linings of worn-out coats. For drummers the knapsack was to have one belt as before, worn over the left shoulder (326).

31 January 1836 - The lower ranks' **greatcoat** was to have nine buttons instead of ten: six along the front opening, two on the shoulder straps, and one on the flaps behind (327).

27 April 1836 - **Lower pompons** [*repeiki*] were ordered to be lined with black leather (328).

13 May 1836 – It was established that girths [*podprugi*] for officers' **saddles** were to be dark green with red stripes (329).

21 October 1836 - Shako **plumes** [*sultany*] were established to be 11 vershoks [19-1/4 inches] high from the triangular hair socket [*tresovka*] to the top, with an upper circumference of 5-2/3 vershoks [10 inches] and a lower one of 4 [7]. Their weight was not to be more than 54 zolotniks [8-1/10 ounces] (330).

14 January 1837 - The wooden parts of the handles of **entrenching tools** [*shantsovyi instrument*] were to be lacquered instead of painted with oil paints. The directives for the fitting and carrying of these tools were confirmed as laid out in detail above for Grenadier regiments (331).

15 July 1837 - A new pattern of officers' **sash** was approved, identical to that introduced to the preceding troops and described above for Grenadier regiments (332).

17 December 1837 - A new pattern of officers' **epaulette** was approved, identical with that introduced at this time in the preceding infantry and cavalry regiments, i.e. with the addition of a fourth twist of thin braid (333).

4 January 1839 - Officers' **pants** were ordered not to have any bows or bands on the front, but were to have them completely smooth in the manner established for lower ranks (334).

16 March 1839 - Lower ranks' **swordbelts** were to be 1-1/2 vershoks [2-3/5 inches] inches wide, while **drummers' crossbelts** were 2-1/2 vershoks [4-2/5 inches] wide as before (335).

16 October 1840 – Rules regarding sewn-on chevrons for lower ranks were confirmed, as set forth above for Guards Lancer regiments (336).

23 January 1841 - The capes of officers' **greatcoats** were to be 1 arshin [28 inches] long as measured from the lower edge of the collar (337).

8 April 1843 – The following changes occurred:
1) Officers and lower ranks were given new model **shakos**, 4-3/4 vershoks [8-3/8 inches] high and curving slightly inward toward the bottom. New dimensions were prescribed for shako plumes: 9-3/4 vershoks [17 inches] high from the hair socket to the top, with an upper circumference of 5-1/4 vershoks [9-3/16 inches] and a lower one of 3-1/2 [6-1/8].
2) It was directed that **drum-majors' epaulettes** [*tambur-mazhorskie epolety*] have red silk between the braided gold thread and in the hanging fringe so as to be more easily distinguished from epaulettes for generals (Illus. 783).
3) **Rank distinctions** for lower ranks in the form of trim [*nashivki*] sewn onto the shoulder straps of coats and greatcoats were established following the scheme prescribed for Army foot artillery, but with Guards tape instead of Army galoon (338).

2 January 1844 - Officers were to have an elongated metallic **cockade** on the forage-cap band, as set forth in detail above for Grenadier regiments (339).

9 May 1844 - Shakos were replaced by **helmets** [*kaski*] of black lacquered leather with two cockades, metal fittings the same color as the buttons, a plume (red for musicians and black for other ranks, of horse hair), and the previous plate, following the pattern introduced for preceding troops (Illus. 784 and 785) (340).

20 May 1844 – Approval was given to a new scheme for differentiating the **forage caps** of lower ranks. Based on this the piping around the upper crown and on both edges of the band was prescribed to be red, while the band itself was black plisse with a cut-out battery number and letter backed by yellow cloth. Officers' cap bands were velvet but, as before, without numbers or letters [341].

7 December 1844 – When in artillery uniform but not on duty, **generals** were to have wear white plumes on their hats [342].

4 January 1845 - Officers' **helmets** were to have a cockade on the right side under the chin-scales [343].

9 August 1845 – When in camp uniform [*lagernaya forma*] **helmets** were ordered to be worn without plumes [344].

19 May 1847 – Lower noncombatant ranks were prescribed **forage caps** the same as in Guards infantry regiments, but with black piping (see Guards Heavy infantry regiments) [345].

29 November 1847 – Distinguished officer candidates [*portupei-praporshchiki i portupei-yunkery*] carrying out the duties of commissioned officers were to wear officers' **half-sabers** [*polusabli*] instead of short swords [*tesaki*] [346].

9 November 1848 - On those days when they were obliged to remain in ceremonial dress [*prazdnichnaya forma*] after the mounting of the guard [*posle razvoda*], generals and field and company-grade officers were permitted to wear the **frock coat** with **helmet** and plume for walking-out [347].

25 April 1848 - The **valise's** flap with buttons was removed [348].

14 September 1849 – Carrying **holsters** for officers' pistols were approved (see Grenadier regiments) [349].

9 and 25 November 1849 – A description of fitting the **helmet** was confirmed (see Grenadier regiments) [350].

17 December 1849 – **Drummers' crossbelts** were to have three grenades on them, as in Guards heavy infantry regiments [351].

24 December 1849 - The grip on the hilt of the **gold half-saber** awarded for bravery was to be gold [352].

17 December 1851 - Approval was given to the manner of gathering up and folding back the skirts of the **greatcoat** (see Grenadier regiments) [353].

8 July 1851 – Approval was given to descriptions of the **drum**, **fife case**, and **water flask** (see Grenadier regiments) [354].

20 October 1851 - A list and description of items to be carried by the soldier in his **knapsack** while on the march and during inspections were confirmed (see Grenadier regiments) [355].

26 January 1852 - Non-combatant lower ranks with grey cloth **forage caps** were to have cloth cap bands of the same color as the collars of combatant personnel [356].

28 December 1852 – For generals, field and company-grade officers, and adjutants, when in formation in campaign dress, an **undress shabrack** [*vitse-cheprak*] was established, of the pattern given on 17 October of this year to Guards infantry regiments [357].

18 February 1854 – A **valise** and **greatcoat** were established for field and company-grade officers (see Grenadier regiments) [358].

29 April 1854 – Generals and field and company-grade offices were to have campaign **greatcoats** in wartime (see Grenadier regiments) [359].

16 June 1854 - The piping around the top of the **forage cap** was to be red in the newly-formed G. Batteries №№4, 5, and 6 [360].

XLIV. GUARDS HORSE ARTILLERY. [*Gvardeiskaya konnaya artilleriya*.]

11 September 1826 – Clerks and in general all non-combatant lower ranks were to have grey **riding-trousers** with red stripes [361].

15 September 1826 - Lower ranks who had completed the regulation number of years of faultless service but who voluntarily remained on active duty were to wear **gold galloon** sewn onto the left sleeve, as described in detail for Grenadier regiments [362].

1 January 1827 - Officers' **epaulettes** were to have small stamped stars as rank distinctions, of the same pattern and scheme as laid out above for Grenadier regiments [363].

31 July 1827 - The numbers and letters on **shako covers** were ordered to be painted with yellow oil paints [364].

8 October 1827 - A new pattern **saber** was approved for lower ranks, straighter than before and with a brass hilt, black grip, and iron scabbard (Illus. 786) [365].

13 October 1827 – Instead of shoulder straps for their coats, combatant lower ranks were given **scaled epaulettes** in the same color as their buttons, with a backing and strap of red cloth (Illus. 786). Together with this the field of officers' epaulettes was also to be scaled [366].

19 November 1827 – Red cloth piping was established for the lower edge of the collar on coats and **greatcoats** [367].

9 February 1828 - A new model **shako** was prescribed, identical with that established at this same time for L.-Gds. Dragoon and Horse-Jäger regiments, but with the pompon and cords in red (silver for officers). The plates on the shako remained as before [368].

24 April 1828 – The changes in the uniforms of **noncombatant non-commissioned officers and craftsmen** were applied, as established for Guards foot artillery and set forth in detail above [369].

20 December 1828 - New pattern **shako badges** were confirmed (of copper for lower ranks, as previously, but gilt for officers), of the pattern established on 24 April 1828 for Guards foot artillery (Illus. 787 and 788) [370].

16 December 1829 - The black cuffs of officers' **frock coats** were changed to dark green, with red piping as before [371].

26 December 1829 - Uniform **buttons** for all ranks were to have a raised representation of a two-headed eagle, as prescribed for the shako plate. In this same year, apart from the dark-green *chakchiry* pants with wide stripes, there were also established **riding trousers** of gray-blue [*sero-sinevatyi*] cloth, with red piping in the side seams [372].

19 July 1831 – On the eagle's shield on buttons and shako plates, **L.-Gds. Horse-Artillery Light Battery №3** was prescribed to have, instead of an image of a Lithuanian horseman, a figure of St. George the Bearer of Victory. From this date the entire Guards horse artillery was to have dress coat buttons on the gray cloth tabs on greatcoat collars (Illus. 789) [373].

28 December 1833 – With the general **reorganization** of the entire Guards Horse Artillery it was ordered to consist of one battery [i.e. heavy] battery and three light, which with their previous uniforms were differentiated only by coat cuff flaps, established as follows: in the Battery and 1st Light batteries—red with white piping; in the 2nd Light Battery—red with dark-green piping; in the 3rd Light Battery—all red. It was also ordered that horse colors were to be by battery: chestnuts in the Battery Battery, sorrels in the 1st Light Battery, blacks in the 2nd Light, and bays in the 3rd Light [374].

13 April 1834 - **Pouches** and **pouch-belts** [*lyadunki i perevyazi*] were to be of a new pattern with a smaller cover and narrower belt [375].

26 April 1834 - **Numbers** and **letters** on the shako covers and forage caps in the Guards horse artillery were to be as follows: in the Battery Battery — Cyrillic *B.B.*, in Light Battery №1 — Cyrillic *1.L.*, and so on. The upper piping of the **forage caps** was to be as before: red in the Battery Battery and white in the Light batteries. The piping on the upper and lower edges of the cap band was red in all batteries, and in between were the same number and letter as prescribed for the shako cover [376].

2 May 1834 - For better handling, the hilts of the **sabers** were to be reworked in a new style as explained above for Dragoon regiments [377].

2 July 1834 - Lower ranks' leather **swordknots** with wool tassels were to be replaced with all-leather ones [378].

31 August 1834 – As in Her Highness's Chevalier Guards and L.-Gds. Horse Regiment, 22 **trumpeters** were authorized for the Guards Horse Artillery [379].

3 December 1834 - Throughout the entire Guards Horse Artillery each man was to have a **pistol**, carried on his person in a special holster [*chushka*] [380].

7 December 1834 - When shakos were worn, the **shako lines** [*snury u kiverov*] were not to reach to the waist, as previously, but only halfway down the back [381].

13 January 1835 - As a reinforcement to the order cited above for 3 December 1834, all mounted trumpeters, non-commissioned officers, and privates were ordered to each have one **pistol** (Illus. 790) [382].

6 April 1835 - All drivers [*yezdovyye*] with the guns and caissons [*zaryadnye yashchiki*] were ordered to have one **pistol** each, after the example of other lower ranks [383].

13 April 1835 - Officers in formation were to use a toggle [*kostylok*] to fasten one end of the **shako lines** [*kivernyi snur*] in back of the shako to an eye-loop [*petlya*] fashioned from the decorative cord [*etishketnyi snur*]. At all other times when officers were not in formation and had to take off the shako, this line was unfastened from the eye-loop and, keeping it around the neck along with its slide [*gaika*], which was to be at the back at the middle of the neck, the end with the toggle was fastened to the second coat lapel button from the top so that the line passed under the right arm and over the pouch-belt [384].

31 January 1836 - Lower ranks' **greatcoats** were to have eleven buttons instead of twelve: six down the front, two on the collar tabs, two on the shoulder straps, and one behind on the flaps [385].

27 April 1836 - **Lower pompons** [*repeiki*] were to be lined with black leather [386].

9 October 1836 - To hold their **pistols**, trumpeters were ordered to have holsters [*chushki*] attached to the saddle on the left side over the saddle cloth. For the cartridges they were to have pouches [*lyadunki*] with crossbelts, like those of other lower ranks (Illus. 791) [387].

17 January 1837 – Rulers were confirmed regarding wearing sabers with the **frock coat**, as set forth above for Guards Lancer regiments [388].

14 February 1837 - Trumpeters, who were prescribed pistols when in mounted formation and cartridge-pouches with belts, were also to wear these **cartridge-pouches** when in dismounted formation [389].

15 July 1837 - A new pattern of officers' **sash** was approved, identical with that introduced at this time for preceding troops and described above (see under the uniforms for grenadier regiments) [390].

17 December 1837 - The new pattern of officers' **epaulettes** was approved, identical with that introduced at this time for preceding troops, i.e. with the addition of a fourth twist of braid [391].

11 January 1838 – Confirmation was given to a description of the **officer's saddle** prescribed for used on 6 March 1834, in all respects in agreement with that laid out above for Army Dragoon regiments [392].

23 February 1838 - Regulations concerning the **pistol holsters** [*pistoletnyya chushki*] mandated for the saddle on 9 October 1836 were confirmed as laid out above for Army Dragoon regiments [393].

4 January 1839 – Generals' and field and company-grade **officers' pants** were not to have any bows or bands in front but rather worn completely smooth and plain in the manner prescribed for lower ranks [394].

16 October 1840 – Confirmation was given to rule concerning **gold chevrons** for lower ranks, as set forth above (see Guards Lancer regiments) [395].

23 January 1841 - The capes of **officers' greatcoats** were to be 1 arshin [28 inches] long as measured from the lower edge of the collar [396].

13 November 1841 - All combatant ranks were given a new pattern **saber** [*sablya*] identical with that introduced at this time for the L.-Gds. Horse-Grenadier and Dragoon regiments, but without a fitting for a bayonet (Illus. 792) [397].

8 April 1843 – A new model **shako** (curving inward towards the bottom), identical to that confirmed for preceding troops (Illus. 793). In order to distinguish between the lower ranks, trimming [*nashivki*] on the **epaulettes** and **shoulder straps** was established on the same basis as prescribed for Foot Artillery [398].

10 May 1843 - Cover flaps [*kryshki*] for **cartridge pouches** were to be (with the cover sewn to the box): 4-1/2 vershoks [8 inches] long, 4-7/8 vershoks [9 inches] wide at the top edge, and 5-5/8 vershoks [10 inches] wide along the bottom edge [399].

2 January 1844 - Officers are to have a **cockade** on the cap band of the forage cap, as described in detail above (see Grenadier regiments) [400].

9 May 1844 - Shakos were replaced by **helmets** with plumes, of the same pattern and in accordance with the same regulations as established for Grenadier Foot Artillery brigades at this time, but with the addition of a metal edging on the front peak, of the same color as the helmet mountings, and with the previous front plate (Illus. 794) [401].

20 May 1844 - Approval was given to a new scheme for differentiating the **forage caps** of lower ranks, according to which the piping around the top and along both edges of the band was to be red. The band was to be of black plisse the battery number and letter cut out and backed by yellow cloth. Officers' cap bands were the same as for lower ranks but, as before, without numbers or letters [402].

4 January 1845 - Officers' **helmets** were to have, on the right side under the chin-scales, a cockade, as set forth above (see preceding troops) (Illus. 795) [403].

9 August 1845 – When in **camp dress, helmets** were ordered to be worn without plumes, even when the personnel concerned were in dress coats (Illus. 795) [404].

4 February 1846 - **Pistols** were abolished for drivers [*yezdovye*] [405].

13 September 1846 – New **holsters** were for officers' percussion lock pistols (see Army Cuirassier regiments) [406].

5 April 1847 – It was ordered that **pistols** be worn in dismounted order in the same way as lancers used to wear them, and that **firing-cap pouches** always be kept in conjuction with the cartridge pouches on their crossbelts [407].

19 May 1847 – Gray **forage caps** with black piping were established for noncombatant lower ranks [408].

9 January 1848 - On those days when they were obliged to remain in ceremonial dress after the mounting of the guard, officers were permitted for walking-out to wear the **frock coat** with *chakchiry* **pants** and **helmets** with **plumes** [409].

19 January 1848 – Approval was given to a description of the **firing-cap pouch** [*kapsulnaya sumochka*] with the cartridge-pouch (see Army Cuirassier regiments) [410].

25 April 1848 - The flap on the **valise** was removed [411].

9 and 25 November 1849 – Approval was given to a description of fitting the **helmet** (see Grenadier regiments) [412].

24 December 1849 – Gold grips were established for the hilts of **gold sabers** awarded for bravery [413].

30 March 1851 - **Cartridge-pouch belts** were to be 1 vershok [1-3/4 inches] wide [414].

15 April 1851 – Confirmation was given to a method of fitting straps to the **valise** for dismounted lower ranks (see Army Cuirassier regiments) [415].

26 January 1852 – It was established that the bands on noncombatant lower ranks' gray **forage caps** were to be the same color as the collar of combatant lower ranks [416].

13 August 1853 - Officers in the campaign dress of **frock coat** without sash were to wear the sword-belt on top of the coat [417].

15 November 1853 – Approval was given to a description of **light cavalry officers' horse furniture** [418].

29 April 1854 – Officers were given campaign **greatcoats** [419].

NOTES

(1) *Collection of Laws and Regulations Relating to the Military Administration*, 1826, Book I, pgs. 108-110.
(2) Actual model saddle cloth preserved in the War Ministry's Commissariat Department.
(3) *Collection of Laws and Regulations*, 1826, Book III, pgs. 255.
(4) Ibid., 1827, Book I, Pt. 3, pg. 109.
(5) Order to the L.-Gds. Hussar Regiment, 17 July 1827.
(6) *Collection of Laws and Regulations*, 1827, Book III, pg. 89.
(7) Information received from the War Ministry's Commissariat Department.
(8) *Collection of Laws and Regulations*, 1827, Book IV, pgs. 17-19.
(9) Ibid., pg. 257.
(10) Ibid., 1828, Book I, pg. 131, and HIGHESTConfirmed models preserved in the War Ministry's Commissariat Department.
(11) *Collection of Laws and Regulations*, 1828, Book II, pg. 131 et seq.
(12) Ibid., Book IV, pg. 47.
(13) Ibid., 1829, Book III, pg. 5.
(14) Ibid., Book IV, pg. 107.
(15) Information received from the War Ministry's Commissariat Department.
(16) *Collection of Laws and Regulations*, 1830, Book III, pg. 217.
(17) Ibid., 1832, Book I, pg. 3.
(18) Information received from the War Ministry's Commissariat Department, and model regimental uniform items preserved there.
(19) *Collection of Laws and Regulations*, 1832, Book III, pg. 329.
(20) Ditto.
(21) From the files of the War Ministry's Commissariat Department.
(22) This change happened upon the renaming of the regiment, without any special order.
(23) *Collection of Laws and Regulations*, 1834, Book II, pg. 233.
(24) Ibid., 1834, Book II, pg. 233.
(25) Ibid., pg. 237.
(26) Ibid., 1834, Book II, pgs. 245-247.
(27) Ibid., pg. 287-290.
(28) Ibid., Book IV, pg. 141.
(29) Ibid., pg. 257.
(30) Ibid., 1835, Book IV, pg. 55.
(31) Ibid., 1835, Book I, pg. 17.
(32) Ibid., pg. 376.
(33) Ibid., 1836, Book I, pgs. 137 and 139.
(34) Ibid., Book II, pg. 171.
(35) Ibid., pg. 173.
(36) Ibid., pg. 209.
(37) Ibid., Book IV, pgs. 153 and 154.
(38) Ibid., 1837, Book I., pg. 133.
(39) Ibid., pg. 55.
(40) Ibid., 1833, Book III, pg. 47.
(41) Ibid., Book IV, pg. 325.
(42) Ibid., 1838, Book I, pgs. 311-315.
(43) Ibid., pg. 329.
(44) Ibid., 1838, Book I., pgs. 337-340.
(45) Ibid., 1839, Book I, pg. 3.
(46) Order of the Minister of War, 16 October 1840, No. 71.
(47) Ditto, 23 January 1841, No. 8.
(48) From the files of the War Ministry's Commissariat Department.
(49) Orders of the Minister of War, 8 April 1843, Nos. 46 and 47.
(50) Ditto, 10 May 1843, Nos. 63 and 64.
(51) Ditto, 2 January 1844, No. 1.
(52) Ditto, 9 May 1844, Nos. 63 and 64.
(53) Ditto, 20 May 1844, No. 69, pgs. 8 and 9.
(54) Ditto, 21 September 1844, No. 115.
(55) Ditto, 17 December 1844, No. 152.
(56) Ditto, 4 January 1845, No. 1.
(57) Ditto, 15 November 1845, No. 139.
(58) Memorandum of the Minister of War to HIS IMPERIAL HIGHNESS the Command-in-Chief of the Guards and Grenadier Corps, 30 April 1846, No. 4162.
(59) Ditto, 5 July 1846, No. 6076.
(60) Order of the Minister of War, 7 August 1846, No. 138.
(61) Ibid., 13 September 1846, No 160.
(62) Ibid., 19 May 1847, No. 86.
(63) Ibid., 31 August 1847, No. 145.
(64) Memorandum of the Minister of War to HIS IMPERIAL HIGHNESS the Command-in-Chief of the Guards and Grenadier Corps, 5 November

1847, No. 10,047.
(65) Order of the Minister of War, 9 January 1848, No. 8.
(66) Ibid., 19 January 1848, No. 17
(67) Ibid., 24 January, 1848, No. 22.
(68) Ibid., 20 February 1848, No. 36.
(69) Ibid., 25 April 1848, No. 80.
(70) Ibid., 24 December 1849, No. 133.
(71) Ibid., 5 March 1850, No. 18.
(72) Ibid., 30 March 1851, No. 36.
(73) Ibid., 15 April, 1851, No. 46.
(74) Ibid., 3 January 1852, No. 2.
(75) Ibid., 26 January 1852, No. 15.
(76) Ibid., 15 November 1853, No. 78.
(77) Ibid., 29 April 1854, No. 53.
(78) *Collection of Laws and Regulations*, 1826, Book I, pgs. 108-110.
(79) Information received from the War Ministry's Commissariat Department.
(80) *Collection of Laws and Regulations*, 1826, Book III, pg. 255.
(81) Ibid., 1827, Book I, pg. 3.
(82) Ibid., Book III, pg. 89.
(83) Information received from the War Ministry's Commissariat Department.
(84) *Collection of Laws and Regulations*, 1827, Book IV, pgs. 17-19.
(85) Ibid., pg. 257, and from the files of the War Ministry's Commissariat Department.
(86) *Collection of Laws and Regulations*, 1828, Book I, pg. 105.
(87) Ibid., pg. 211.
(88) Ibid., Book II, pg. 131 et seq.
(89) Ibid., 1829, Book III, pg. 5.
(90) Ibid., Book IV, pg. 115.
(91) Information received from the War Ministry's Commissariat Department.
(92) *Collection of Laws and Regulations*, 1830, Book III, pg. 217.
(93) Information received from the War Ministry's Commissariat Department.
(94) *Collection of Laws and Regulations*, 1832, Book I, pg. 3.
(95) Order of the Minister of War, 22 February 1833, No. 18.
(96) *Collection of Laws and Regulations*, 1834, Book II, pg. 237.
(97) Ibid., pgs. 245-247.
(98) Ibid., Book IV, pg. 141.
(99) Ibid., 1835, Book. I, pg. 317.
(100) Ibid., Book III, pgs 175-178.
(101) Ibid., 1836, Book I, pgs. 137 and 139.
(102) Ibid., Book IV, pgs. 153 and 154.
(103) Ibid., 1837, Book I, pg. 133.
(104) Ibid., pg. 55.
(105) Ibid., pg. 123.
(106) Ibid., Book III, pg. 89.
(107) Ibid., pg. 47.
(108) Ibid., pg. 65.
(109) Ibid., Book IV, pg. 325.
(110) Ibid., 1838, Book I, pgs. 311-315.
(111) Ibid., pg. 329.
(112) Ibid., 1839, Book I, pg. 3.
(113) Order of the Minister of War, 16 October 1840, No. 60.
(114) Ibid., 23 January 1841, No. 8.
(115) Ibid., 31 January 1843, No. 16.
(116) Ibid., 8 April 1843, No. 46.
(117) Ibid., 10 May 1843, Nos. 63 and 64.
(118) Ibid., 2 January 1844, No. 1
(119) Ibid., 19 February 1844, No. 16.
(120) Ibid., 20 May 1844, No. 69.
(121) Ibid., 21 September 1844, No. 115.
(122) Ibid., 19 November 1845, No. 140.
(123) Ibid., 17 August 1846, No. 138.
(124) Ibid., 13 September 1846, No. 160.
(125) Ibid., 19 May 1847, No. 86.
(126) Ibid., 9 January 1848, No. 8.
(127) Ibid., 19 January 1848, No. 17.
(128) Ibid., 25 April 1848, No. 80.
(129) Ibid., 7 November 1849, No. 111.
(130) Ibid., 24 December 1849, No. 133.

(131) Ibid., 5 March 1850, No. 18.
(132) Ibid., 3 February 1851, No. 12.
(133) Ibid., 30 March 1851, No. 36.
(134) Ibid., 15 April 1851, No. 46.
(135) Ibid., 3 January 1852, No. 2.
(136) Ibid., 26 January 1852, No. 15.
(137) Ibid., 16 July 1852, No. 81.
(138) Ibid., 13 August 1853, No. 61.
(139) Ibid., 18 February 1854, No. 21.
(140) Ibid., 29 April 1854, No. 53.
(141) *Collection of Laws and Regulations*, 1826, Book I, pgs. 108-110, and model sabertache and saddlecloth preserved in the War Ministry's Commissariat Department.
(142) From the files of the War Ministry's Commissariat Department.
Collection of Laws and Regulations, 1826, Book III, pg. 255.
(144) Ibid., 1827, Book I, pg. 3.
(145) Ibid., Book I, pg. 155.
(146) Order to the L.-Gds. Hussar Regiment.
(147) *Collection of Laws and Regulations*, 1827, Book III, pg. 75.
(148) Ibid., pg. 89.
(149) Ibid., Book IV, pgs. 17-19.
(150) Ibid., pg. 257.
(151) Ibid., 1828, Book II, pgs. 131 et seq.
(152) Ibid., 1829, Book II. pg. 5
(153) Ibid., Book IV, pg. 107.
(154) Ibid., 1832, Book I. pg. 3.
(155) Information received from the War Ministry's Commissariat Department.
(156) *Collection of Laws and Regulations*, 1833, Book IV, pg. 107.
(157) Ibid., 1834, Book II, pg. 237.
(158) Ibid., pgs. 245-247.
(159) Ibid., Book IV, pg. 141.
(160) Ibid., pg. 257.
(161) Ibid., 1835, Book I, pg. 117.
(162) Ibid., pg. 367.
(163) Ibid., Book II, pg. 283.
(164) Ibid., Book III, pg. 175-178, and notification by the Commander of the L.-Gds. Hussar Regiment dated 6 November 1846, No. 2241.
(165) *Collection of Laws and Regulations*, 1836, Book I, pg. 137.
(166) Ibid., Book II, pg. 209.
(167) Ibid., Book IV, pg. 153.
(168) Ibid., 1837, Book I, pg. 55.
(169) Ibid., pg. 123.
(170) Ibid., Book IV, pg. 325.
(171) Ibid., 1838, Book I, pg. 329.
(172) Ibid., Book II, pg. 423.
(173) Ibid., 1839, Book I, pg. 3.
(174) Order of the Minister of War, 16 October 1840, No. 71.
(175) Ibid., 23 January 1841, No. 8.
(176) Ibid., 8 April 1843, Nos. 46 and 47.
(177) Ibid., 10 May 1843, Nos. 63 and 64.
(178) Ibid., 2 January 1844, No. 1
(179) Ibid., 19 February 1844, No. 16.
(180) Ibid., 20 May 1844, No. 69, pgs. 10 and 11.
(181) Ibid., 21 September 1844, No. 115.
(182) Ibid., 17 December 1844, No. 155.
(183) Ibid., 27 January 1845, No. 18.
(184) Ibid., 26 February 1845, No. 35.
(185) Ibid., 15 April 1845, No. 67.
(186) Ibid., 18 August 1845, No. 106.
(187) Ibid., 8 September 1845, No. 111.
(188) Ibid., 15 November 1845, No. 139.
(189) Ibid., 7 August 1846, No. 138.
(190) Ibid., 13 September 1846, No. 160.
(191) Memorandum from the Commissariat Department to the War Ministry's Inspection Department, 26 October 1846, No. 8572.
(192) Order of the Minister of War, 19 May 1847, No. 86.
(193) Ibid., 9 January 1848, No. 8.
(194) Ibid., 19 January 1848, No. 17.
(195) Ibid., 25 April 1848, No. 80.
(196) Ibid., 17 December 1849, No. 130.

(197) Ibid., 24 December 1849, No. 133.
(198) Ibid., 5 March 1850, No. 18.
(199) Ibid., 3 February 1851, No. 12.
(200) Ibid., 30 March 1851, No. 36.
(201) Ibid., 3 January 1852, No. 2
(202) Ibid., 26 January 1852, No. 15.
(203) Ibid., 12 July 1852, No. 76.
(204) Ibid., 16 July 1852, No. 81.
(205) Ibid., 29 August 1852, No. 97.
(206) Ibid., 3 January 1853, No. 3.
(207) Ibid., 13 August 1853, No. 61.
(208) Ibid., 15 November 1853, No. 78.
(209) Ibid., 18 February 1854, No. 21.
(210) Ibid., 29 April 1854, No. 53.
(211) *Collection of Laws and Regulations*, 1826, Book II, pg. 183.
(212) Ibid., Book III, pg. 255.
(213) Ibid., Book IV, pg. 103.
(214) Ibid., 1827, Book I, pg. 3.
(215) From the files of the War Ministry's Commissariat Department.
(216) *Collection of Laws and Regulations*, 1827, Book II, pg. 279.
(217) Ibid., Book IV, pg. 257.
(218) Ibid., 1828, Book I, pg. 211.
(219) Ibid., 1829, Book III, pg. 5.
(220) Ibid., Book IV, pg. 115.
(221) Ibid., 1832, Book II, pg. 545.
(222) Ibid., 1834, Book II, pg. 237.
(223) Ibid., pgs. 245-247.
(224) Ibid., 1835, Book I, pg. 365.
(225) Ibid., pg. 319.
(226) Ibid., pg. 245.
(227) Ibid., Book III, pg. 145.
(228) Ibid., 1836, Book I, pgs. 137 and 139.
(229) Ibid., Book IV, pgs. 153 and 154.
(230) Ibid., 1837, Book I, pg. 133.
(231) Ibid., pg. 55.
(232) Ibid., 1837, Book III, pg. 47.
(233) Ibid., Book IV, pg. 325.
(234) Ibid., 1838, Book I, pgs. 311-315.
(235) Ibid., pg. 329.
(236) Ibid., 1839, Book I, pg. 3.
(237) Order of the Minister of War, 16 October 1840, No. 60.
(238) Ibid., 23 January 1841, No. 8.
(239) Ibid., 8 April 1843, No. 44 § 6.
(240) Ibid., 8 April 1843, No. 46.
(241) Ibid., 10 May 1843, Nos. 63 and 64.
(242) Ibid., 2 January 1844, No. 1.
(243) Ibid., 27 January 1845, No. 17.
(244) Ibid., 7 August 1846, No. 138.
(245) Ibid., 13 September 1846, No. 160.
(246) Ibid., 9 January 1848, No. 8.
(247) Ibid., 25 April 1848, No. 80.
(248) Ibid., 24 December 1849, No. 133.
(249) Ibid., 30 March 1851, No. 36.
(250) Ibid., 13 August 1853, No. 61.
(251) Ibid., 15 November 1853, No. 78.
(252) Ibid., 18 February 1854, No. 21.
(253) Ibid., 29 April 1854, No. 53.
(254) *Collection of Laws and Regulations*, 1826, Book III, pg. 255.
(255) Ibid., 1827, Book I, pg. 3.
(256) Information received from the War Ministry's Commissariat Department.
(257) *Collection of Laws and Regulations*, 1827, Book IV, pgs. 17-19, and from the files of the War Ministry's Commissariat Department.
(258) *Collection of Laws and Regulations*, 1827, Book IV, pg. 257.
(259) Ibid., 1828, Book I, pg. 211.
(260) Ibid., 1829, Book I, pg. 241.
(261) Information received from the War Ministry's Commissariat Department.
(262) *Collection of Laws and Regulations*, 1829, Book IV, pg. 19.
(263) Ibid., pg. 118.

(264) Ibid., 1830, Book I, pg. 13.
(265) Information received from the War Ministry's Commissariat Department.
(266) The same information.
(267) *Complete Collection of Laws of the Russian Empire, Collection 2* [Polnoe Sobranie Zakonov Rossiiskoi Imperii--hereafter PSZ], Vol. VI, sec. 2, No. 4861, § 7.
(268) Information received from the War Ministry's Commissariat Department.
(269) Information received from the same Department.
(270) *Collection of Laws and Regulations*, 1834, Book II, pgs. 245-247.
(271) Ibid., Book IV, pg. 257.
(272) Information received from the War Ministry's Commissariat Department.
(273) *Collection of Laws and Regulations*, 1835, Book II, pg. 283.
(274) Ibid., 1836, Book I, pg. 137 and 139.
(275) Ibid., Book II, pg. 171.
(276) Ibid., 1837, Book I, pg. 133.
(277) Ibid., Book III, pg. 47.
(278) Ibid., Book IV, pg. 325.
(279) Ibid., 1838, Book I, pgs. 311-315.
(280) Ibid., 1839, Book I, pg. 3.
(281) Ibid., Book III, pg. 41.
(282) Order of the Minister of War, 16 October 1840, No. 60.
(283) Ibid., 29 October 1840, No. 75.
(284) Ibid., 23 January 1841, No. 8.
(285) Ibid., 8 April 1843, No. 44 §§ 11, 46, and 47.
(286) Ibid., 2 January 1844, No. 1.
(287) Ibid., 12 April 1844, No. 48.
(288) Ibid., 9 May 1844, Nos. 63 and 64.
(289) Ibid., 20 May 1844, No. 69, pgs. 20 and 21.
(290) Ibid., 23 September 1844, No. 116.
(291) Ibid., 4 January 1845, No. 1.
(292) Ibid., 19 May 1847, No. 86.
(293) Ibid., 9 January 1848, No. 8.
(294) Ibid., 25 April 1848, No. 80.
(295) Ibid., 17 April 1852, No. 43.
(296) Ibid., 13 August 1853, No. 61.
(297) Ibid., 18 February 1854, No. 21.
(298) Ibid., 29 April 1854, No. 53.
(299) *Collection of Laws and Regulations*, 1826, Book I, pgs. 185, 108 §6, and 110.
(300) Ibid., Book II, pg. 47.
(301) Ibid., Book III, pg. 255.
(302) Ibid., Book IV, pg. 95.
(303) Ibid., 1827, Book I, pg. 3.
(304) Ibid., pg. 153.
(305) Ibid., pg. 249.
(306) Ibid., Book III, pg. 89.
(307) Ibid., Book IV, pg. 267.
(308) Ibid., 1828, Book I, pg. 211.
(309) Ibid., Book II, pgs. 131 et seq.
(310) Ibid., 1829, Book II, pg. 221 §12.
(311) Ibid., Book IV, pg. 127.
(312) Ibid., pg. 107.
(313) Ibid., pg. 115, and information received from the War Ministry's Commissariat Department.
(314) Information received from the same Department.
(315) Order of the Chief of HIS IMPERIAL MAJESTY'S Main Staff, 1 January 1832, No. 1.
(316) *Collection of Laws and Regulations*, 1832, Book II, pg. 545.
(317) Ibid., 1833, Book I, pg. 419.
(318) Ibid., pg. 463.
(319) Information received from the War Ministry's Commissariat Department.
(320) Ditto.
(321) Information received from the War Ministry's Artillery Department, and a HIGHEST Confirmed model short sword.
(322) *Collection of Laws and Regulations*, 1834, Book II, pg. 243.
(323) Ibid., pg. 257.
(324) Ibid., pg. 163.
(325) Ibid., Book III, pg. 465.
(326) Ibid., 1835, Book III, pg. 179.
(327) Ibid., 1836, Book I, pg. 137.
(328) Information received from the War Ministry's Commissariat Department.
(329) *Collection of Laws and Regulations*, 1836, Book II, pg. 171.
(330) Ibid., Book IV, pg. 157.

(331) Ibid., 1837, Book I, pg. 353.
(332) Ibid., Book III, pg. 47.
(333) Ibid., Book IV, pg. 325.
(334) Ibid., 1839, Book I, pg. 3.
(335) Ibid., pg. 179.
(336) Order of the Minister of War, 16 October 1840, No. 60.
(337) Ibid., 23 January 1841, No. 8.
(338) Ibid., 8 April 1843, Nos. 44 and 46.
(339) Ibid., 2 January 1844, No. 1.
(340) Ibid., 9 May 1844, Nos. 63 and 64.
(341) Ibid., 20 May 1844, No. 69.
(342) Ibid., 7 December 1844, No. 147.
(343) Ibid., 4 January 1845, No. 1.
(344) Ibid., 9 August 1845, No. 101.
(345) Ibid., 19 May 1847, No. 86.
(346) Ibid., 29 November 1847, No. 186.
(347) Ibid., 9 January 1848, No. 8.
(348) Ibid., 25 April 1848, No. 80.
(349) Ibid., 14 September 1849, No. 88.
(350) Ibid., 9 and 25 November 1849, Nos. 110 and 117.
(351) Ibid., 17 December 1849, No. 129.
(352) Ibid., 24 December 1849, No. 133.
(353) Ibid., 17 January 1851, No. 7.
(354) Ibid., 13 December 1851, No. 134.
(355) Ibid., 20 October 1851, No. 120.
(356) Ibid., 26 January 1852, No. 15.
(357) Ibid., 28 December 1852, No. 147.
(358) Ibid., 18 February 1854, No. 21.
(359) Ibid., 29 April 1854, No. 53.
(360) Ibid., 16 July 1854, No. 65.
(361) *Collection of Laws and Regulations*, 1826, Book I, pgs. 108-110.
(362) Ibid., Book III, pg. 255.
(363) Ibid., 1827, Book I, pg. 3.
(364) Ibid., Book III, pg. 89.
(365) Information received from the War Ministry's Commissariat Department.
(366) *Collection of Laws and Regulations*, 1827, Book IV, pgs. 17-19.
(367) Ibid., pg. 267.
(368) Ibid., 1828, Book I, pg. 131.
(369) Ibid., Book II, pgs. 131 et seq.
(370) Ibid., Book IV, pg. 47.
(371) Ibid., 1829, Book IV, pg. 107.
(372) Ibid., pg. 115.
(373) Information received from the War Ministry's Commissariat Department.
(374) Ditto.
(375) Ditto.
(376) *Collection of Laws and Regulations*, 1834, Book II, pg. 243.
(377) Ibid., pgs. 245-247.
(378) Ibid., Book III, pg. 433.
(379) Ibid., Book II, pg. 422.
(380) Ibid., Book IV, pg. 141.
(381) Ibid., pg. 257.
(382) Ibid., 1835, Book I, pg. 317.
(383) Ibid., Book II, pg. 275.
(384) Ibid., pg. 283.
(385) Ibid., 1836, Book I, pg. 137.
(386) Ibid., Book II, pg. 171.
(387) Ibid., Book IV, pgs. 153 and 154.
(388) Ibid., 1837, Book I, pg. 133.
(389) Ibid., pg. 55.
(390) Ibid., Book III, pg. 47.
(391) Ibid., Book IV, pg. 325.
(392) Ibid., 1838, Book I, pgs. 311-315.
(393) Ibid., pg. 329.
(394) Ibid., 1839, Book I, pg. 3.
(395) Order of the Minister of War, 16 October 1840, No. 60.
(396) Ibid., 25 January 1841, No. 8.
(397) Information received from the War Ministry's Artillery Department, and a HIGHEST Confirmed model saber.

(398) Order of the Minister of War, 8 April 1843, Nos. 44 and 46.
(399) Ibid., 10 May 1843, No. 63.
(400) Ibid., 2 January 1844, No. 1.
(401) Ibid., 9 May 1844, Nos. 63 and 64.
(402) Ibid., 20 May 1844, No. 69.
(403) Ibid., 4 January 1845, No. 1.
(404) Ibid., 9 August 1845, No. 101.
(405) Ibid., 4 February 1846, No. 30.
(406) Ibid., 13 September 1846, No. 160.
(407) Memorandum of the Duty General of HIS IMPERIAL MAJESTY'S Main Staff to the War Ministry's Commissariat Department, 5 Apri 1847, No. 3082.
(408) Order of the Minister of War, 19 May 1847, No. 86.
(409) Ibid., 9 January 1848, No. 8.
(410) Ibid., 19 January 1848, No. 17.
(411) Ibid., 25 April 1848, No. 80.
(412) Ibid., 9 and 25 November 1849, Nos. 110 and 117.
(413) Ibid., 24 December 1849, No. 133.
(414) Ibid., 30 March 1851, No. 36.
(415) Ibid., 15 April 1851, No. 46.
(416) Ibid., 26 January 1852, No. 15.
(417) Ibid., 13 August 1853, No. 61.
(418) Ibid., 15 November 1853, No. 78.
(419) Ibid., 29 April 1854, No. 53.

PLATES LIST OF ILLUSTRATIONS

705. Company-Grade Officer and Non-Commissioned Officer. L.-Gds. Dragoon Regiment, 1827.
706. Company-Grade Officer and Trumpeter. L.-Gds. Horse-Jäger Regiment, 1828-1831.
707. Private and Company-Grade Officer. L.-Gds. Dragoon Regiment, 1828-1832.
708. Trumpeter and Private. L.-Gds. Horse-Jäger Regiment, 1831-1833.
709. Lower ranks' helmet in the L.-Gds. Horse-Grenadier Regiment, established 10 January 1832.
710. Trumpeter, NCO and Company-Grade Officer. L.-Gds. Horse-Grenadier Regiment, 1832-1841.
711. Drummer. L.-Gds. Horse-Grenadier Regiment, 1832-1841.
712. Field-Grade Officer and Private. L.-Gds. Dragoon Regiment, 1833-1841.
713. Private. L.-Gds. Horse-Grenadier Regiment, 1834-1841
714. Company-Grade Officers. L.-Gds. Dragoon Regiment, 1835-1841
715. Trumpeter. L.-Gds. Horse-Grenadier Regiment, 1836-1841.
716. Field-Grade Officer and Private. L.-Gds. Horse-Grenadier Regiment, 1841-1848.
717. Private. L.-Gds. Dragoon Regiment, 1841-1843.
718. Drummer. L.-Gds. Dragoon Regiment, 1843-1844.
719. Private and Trumpeter. L.-Gds. Dragoon Regiment, 1844-1848.
720. Company-Grade Officer. L.-Gds. Dragoon Regiment, 1844-1848.
721. Company-Grade Officer. L.-Gds. Dragoon Regiment, 1845-1848.
722. Field-Grade Officer. L.-Gds. Horse-Grenadier Regiment, 1846-1848.
723. Private. L.-Gds. Horse-Grenadier Regiment, 1848-1855.
724. Company-Grade Officer. L.-Gds. Dragoon Regiment, 1848-1855.
725. Private. L.-Gds. Lancer Regiment, 1826-1827.
726. Trumpeter. L.-Gds. Lancer Regiment, 1827-1837.
727. NCO. His Imperial highness Gran Duke Constantine Pavlovich's L.-Gds. Lancer Regiment, 1827-1831.
728. Cy-Grade Officer. His Imperial highness Gran Duke Constantine Pavlovich's L.-Gds. Lancer Regiment, 1828-1837.
729. Company-Grade Officer. His Imperial highness Gran Duke Micael Pavlovich's L.-Gds. Lancer Regiment, 1831-1837.
730. Non-Commissioned Officer. L.-Gds. Lancer Regiment, 1835-1836.
731. Trumpeter. His Imperial highness Gran Duke Micael Pavlovich's L.-Gds. Lancer Regiment, 1836-1846.
732. Private. L.-Gds. Lancer Regiment, 1837-1846.
733. Non-Commissioned Officer and Company-Grade Officer. L.-Gds. Lancer Regiment, 1837-1846.
734. Private. L.-Gds. Lancer Regiment, 1844-1855.
735. Private. L.-Gds. Lancer Regiment, 1846-1855.
736. Officer's sabertache, L.-Gds. Hussar Regiment, 1826-1855.
737. Officer's saddlecloth, L.-Gds. Hussar Regiment, 1826-1855.
738. Private. L.-Gds. Hussar Regiment, 1826-1835.
739. Field-Grade Officer. L.-Gds. Hussar Regiment, 1826-1835.
740. Company-Grade Officers. L.-Gds. Hussar Reg. and L.-Gds. Grodno Hussar Regiment, 1826-1833.
741. Privates. L.-Gds. Hussar Regiment, 1827-1829.
742. Company-Grade Officer and Non-Commissioned Officer. L.-Gds. Grodno Hussar Reg., 1832.
743. Private. L.-Gds. Grodno Hussar Regiment, 1833-1835.
744. Company-Grade Officer. L.-Gds. Grodno Hussar Regiment, 1833-1835.
745. Private and Field-Grade Officers. L.-Gds. Grodno Hussar Regiment, 1833-1845.
746. Field-Grade Officer, L.-Gds. Hussar Reg., and Private, L.-Gds. Grodno Hussar Reg., 1835-1838.
747. Trumpeter. L.-Gds. Hussar Regiment, 1836-1838.
748. Private, L.-Gds. Hussar Regiment, and Company-Grade Officer, L.-Gds. Grodno Hussar Regiment, 1838-1843.
749. Company-Grade Officer. L.-Gds. Hussar Regiment, 1843-1845.
750. General. L.-Gds. Hussar Regiment, 1844-1855.
751. Headdress for Guards Hussar regiments, established 27 January 1845.

752. Company-Grade officer, L.-Gds. Hussar Regiment, and Trumpeter, L.-Gds. Grodno Hussar Regiment, 1845-1855.
753. Company-Grade officers. L.-Gds. Hussar and L.-Gds. Grodno Hussar Regiments, 1845-1852.
754. Company-Grade officers. L.-Gds. Hussar and L.-Gds. Grodno Hussar Regiments, 1845-1855.
755. General. L.-Gds. Hussar Regiment, 1846-1855.
756. Privates. L.-Gds. Hussar and L.-Gds. Grodno Hussar Regiments, 1849-1855.
757. Field-Grade Officer. L.-Gds. Hussar Regiment, 1852-1855.
758. Company-Grade Officer. L.-Gds. Grodno Hussar Regiment, 1854-1855.
759. Company-Grade Officer and Private. L.-Gds. Gendarme Half-Squadron, 1826-1827.
760. Trumpeter. L.-Gds. Gendarme Half-Squadron, 1827-1829.
761. Company-Grade Officers. L.-Gds. Gendarme Half-Squadron, 1827-1829.
762. Private. L.-Gds. Gendarme Half-Squadron, 1835-1843.
763. Company-Grade Officer and Trumpeter. L.-Gds. Gendarme Half-Squadron, 1845-1855.
764. Company-Grade Officer and Private. L.-Gds. Gendarme Half-Squadron, 1845-1855.
765. Private and Company-Grade Officer. Train of the Guards troops under the command of HIS IMPERIAL HIGHNESS TESAREVICH CONSTANTINE PAVLOVICH, 1827-1829.
766. Company-Grade Officer and Private. Guards Train, 1829.
767. Non-Commissioned Officer. Guards Train, 1829-1843.
768. Company-Grade Officer. Guards Train, 1843-1844.
769. Private. Guards Train, 1844-1849.
770. Company-Grade Officer. Guards Train, 1845-1849.
771. Private [*Kanonir*], 1st Guards Artillery Brigade, and Company-Grade Officer, 2nd Guards Artillery Brigade. 1826-1827.
772. Non-Commissioned Officer [*Feierverker*], L.-Gds. Battery Battery No. 5, 1826-1828.
773. Field-Grade Officer. 1st Guards Artillery Brigade. 1826-1828.
774. Drummer. 2nd Guards Artillery Brigade, 1827.
775. Bombardier. 1st. Guards Artillery Brigade, 1828-1833.
776. Field-Grade Officer. 2nd Guards Artillery Brigade, 1828-1843.
777. Non-commissioned Officer [*Feierverker*] and Company-Grade Officer. 1st Guards Artillery Brigade, 1833-1843.
778. Company-Grade Officer and Drummer. 2nd Guards Artillery Brigade, 1833.
779. Company-Grade Officer and Bombardier. 6th Battery Battery of the 3rd Guards and Grenadier Artillery Brigade, 1833.
780. Company-Grade Officer. 3rd Light Battery of the 3rd Guards and Grenadier Artillery Brigade, 1833-1843.
781. Bombardier. Grenadier batteries of the 3rd Guards and Grenadier Artillery Brigade, 1834-1843.
782. Non-commissioned Officer [*Feierverker*]. 1st Guards Artillery Brigade, 1834-1843.
783. Drum-Major. 1st Guards Artillery Brigade, 1843-1844.
784. Company-Grade Officer, 1st Guards Artillery Brigade, and Drummer, 2nd Guards Artillery Brigade. 1844-1849.
785. Company-Grade Officer of the 6th Battery Battery, and Cannoneer and Company-Grade Officer of the 3rd Light Battery, 3rd Guards and Grenadier Artillery Brigade, 1844-1849.
786. Cannoneer. Guards Horse Artillery, 1827.
787. Non-commissioned Officer [*Feierverker*]. Guards Horse Artillery, 1828-1841.
788. Company-Grade Officer. Guards Horse Artillery, 1828-1843.
789. Cannoneer. Guards Horse Artillery, 1831-1855.
790. Bombardier. Guards Horse Artillery, 1835-1841.
791. Trumpeter. Guards Horse Artillery, 1836-1843.
792. Bombardier. Guards Horse Artillery, 1841-1843.
793. Company-Grade Officer. Guards Horse Artillery, 1843-1844.
794. Company-Grade Officer and Trumpeter. Guards Horse Artillery, 1844-1849.
795. General. Guards Horse Artillery, 1845-1849.

Company-Grade Officer and Non-Commissioned Officer. L.-Gds. Dragoon Regiment, 1827.

706

Company-Grade Officer and Trumpeter. L.-Gds. Horse-Jäger Regiment, 1828-1831.

Private and Company-Grade Officer. L.-Gds. Dragoon Regiment, 1828-1832.

708

Trumpeter and Private. L.-Gds. Horse-Jäger Regiment, 1831-1833.

709

Lower ranks' helmet in the L.-Gds. Horse-Grenadier Regiment, established 10 January 1832.

710

Trumpeter, Non-Commissioned Officer, and Company-Grade Officer. L.-Gds. Horse-Grenadier Regiment, 1832-1841.

711

Drummer. L.-Gds. Horse-Grenadier Regiment, 1832-1841.

712

Field-Grade Officer and Private. L.-Gds. Dragoon Regiment, 1833-1841.

713

Private. L.-Gds. Horse-Grenadier Regiment, 1834-1841

714

Company-Grade Officers. L.-Gds. Dragoon Regiment, 1835-1841.

Trumpeter. L.-Gds. Horse-Grenadier Regiment, 1836-1841.

716

Field-Grade Officer and Private. L.-Gds. Horse-Grenadier Regiment, 1841-1848.

717

Private. L.-Gds. Dragoon Regiment, 1841-1843.

718

Drummer. L.-Gds. Dragoon Regiment, 1843-1844.

Private and Trumpeter. L.-Gds. Dragoon Regiment, 1844-1848.

720

Company-Grade Officer. L.-Gds. Dragoon Regiment, 1844-1848.

721

Company-Grade Officer. L.-Gds. Dragoon Regiment, 1845-1848.

722

Field-Grade Officer. L.-Gds. Horse-Grenadier Regiment, 1846-1848.

Private. L.-Gds. Horse-Grenadier Regiment, 1848-1855.

724

Company-Grade Officer. L.-Gds. Dragoon Regiment, 1848-1855.

725

Private. L.-Gds. Lancer Regiment, 1826-1827.

726

Trumpeter. L.-Gds. Lancer Regiment, 1827-1837.

Non-Commissioned Officer. L.-Gds. Lancer Regiment, 1827-1831.

728

Company-Grade Officer. L.-Gds. Lancer Regiment, 1828-1837.

729

Company-Grade Officer. L.-Gds. Lancer Regiment, 1831-1837.

730

Non-Commissioned Officer. L.-Gds. Lancer Regiment, 1835-1836.

731

Trumpeter. L.-Gds. Lancer Regiment, 1836-1846.

732

Private. L.-Gds. Lancer Regiment, 1837-1846.

Non-Commissioned Officer and Company-Grade Officer. L.-Gds. Lancer Regiment, 1837-1846.

734

Private. L.-Gds. Lancer Regiment, 1844-1855.

735

Private. L.-Gds. Lancer Regiment, 1846-1855.

Officer's sabertache, L.-Gds. Hussar Regiment, 1826-1855.

737

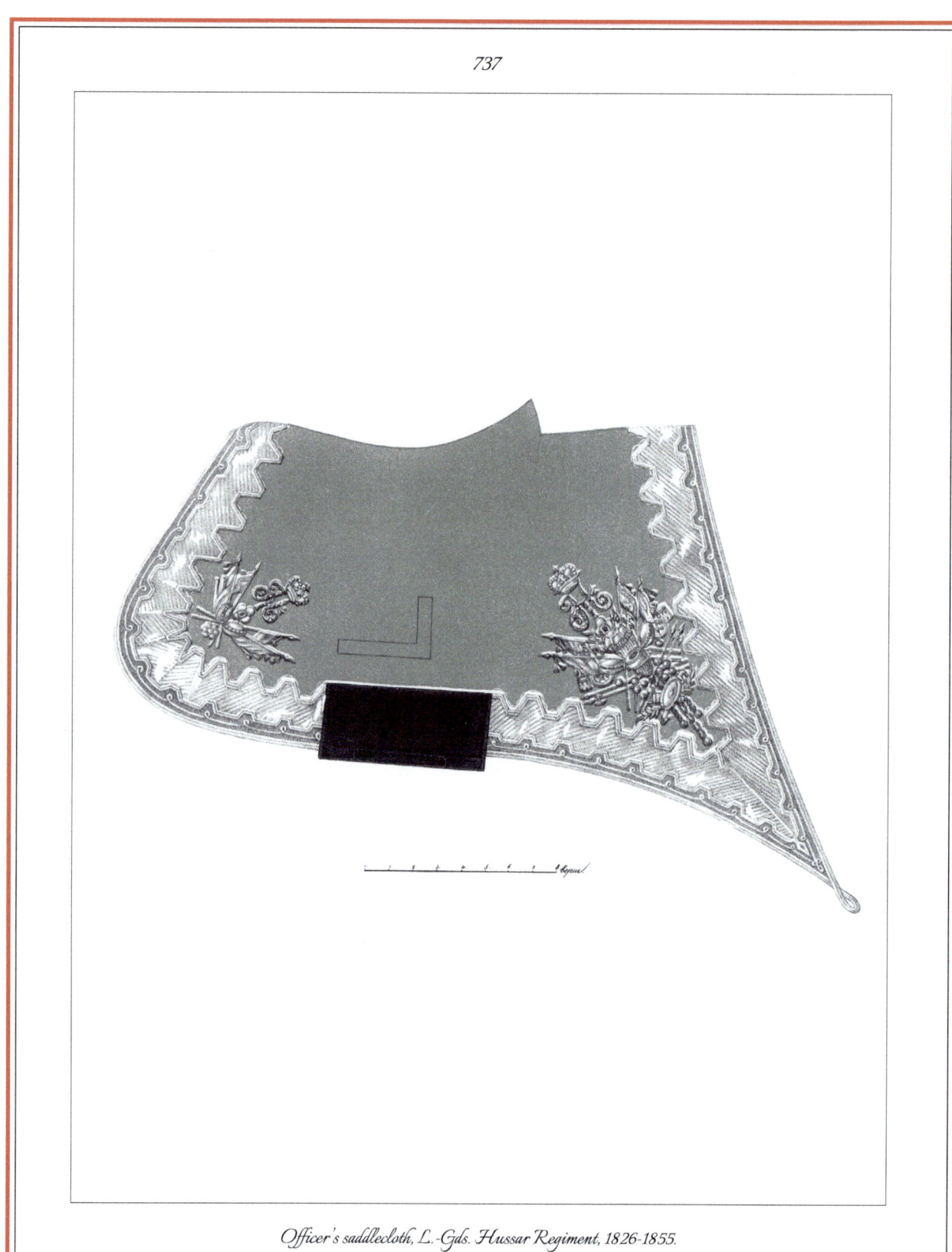

Officer's saddlecloth, L.-Gds. Hussar Regiment, 1826-1855.

Private. L.-Gds. Hussar Regiment, 1826-1835.

739

Field-Grade Officer. L.-Gds. Hussar Regiment, 1826-1835.

740

Company-Grade Officers. L.-Gds. Hussar Regiment and L.-Gds. Grodno Hussar Regiment, 1826-1833.

741

Privates. L.-Gds. Hussar Regiment, 1827-1829.

Company-Grade Officer and Non-Commissioned Officer. L.-Gds. Grodno Hussar Regiment, 1832.

Private. L.-Gds. Grodno Hussar Regiment, 1833-1835.

Company-Grade Officer. L.-Gds. Grodno Hussar Regiment, 1833-1835.

745

Private and Field-Grade Officers. L.-Gds. Grodno Hussar Regiment, 1833-1845.

746

Field-Grade Officer, L.-Gds. Hussar Regiment, and Private, L.-Gds. Grodno Hussar Regiment, 1835-1838.

747

Trumpeter. L.-Gds. Hussar Regiment, 1836-1838.

Private, L.-Gds. Hussar Regiment, and Company-Grade Officer, L.-Gds. Grodno Hussar Regiment, 1838-1843.

749

Company-Grade Officer. L.-Gds. Hussar Regiment, 1843-1845.

750

General. L.-Gds. Hussar Regiment, 1844-1855.

751

Headdress for Guards Hussar regiments, established 27 January 1845.

752

Company-Grade officer, L.-Gds. Hussar Regiment, and Trumpeter, L.-Gds. Grodno Hussar Regiment, 1845-1855.

Company-Grade officers. L.-Gds. Hussar and L.-Gds. Grodno Hussar Regiments, 1845-1852.

754

Company-Grade officers. L.-Gds. Hussar and L.-Gds. Grodno Hussar Regiments, 1845-1855.

General. L.-Gds. Hussar Regiment, 1846-1855.

756

Privates. L.-Gds. Hussar and L.-Gds. Grodno Hussar Regiments, 1849-1855.

757

Field-Grade Officer. L.-Gds. Hussar Regiment, 1852-1855.

758

Company-Grade Officer. L.-Gds. Grodno Hussar Regiment, 1854-1855.

759

Company-Grade Officer and Private. L.-Gds. Gendarme Half-Squadron, 1826-1827.

760

Trumpeter. L.-Gds. Gendarme Half-Squadron, 1827-1829.

Company-Grade Officers. L.-Gds. Gendarme Half-Squadron, 1827-1829.

Private. L.-Gds. Gendarme Half-Squadron, 1835-1843.

Company-Grade Officer and Trumpeter. L.-Gds. Gendarme Half-Squadron, 1845-1855.

Company-Grade Officer and Private. L.-Gds. Gendarme Half-Squadron, 1845-1855.

765

Private and Company-Grade Officer, 1827-1829.

766

Company-Grade Officer and Private. Guards Train, 1829.

Non-Commissioned Officer. Guards Train, 1829-1843.

768

Company-Grade Officer. Guards Train, 1843-1844.

769

Private. Guards Train, 1844-1849.

770

Company-Grade Officer. Guards Train, 1845-1849.

771

Private [Kanonir], 1st Guards Artillery Brigade, and Company-Grade Officer, 2nd Guards Artillery Brigade. 1826-1827.

772

Non-Commissioned Officer [Feierverker], L.-Gds. Battery Battery No. 5, 1826-1828.

773

Field-Grade Officer. 1st Guards Artillery Brigade. 1826-1828.

774

Drummer. 2nd Guards Artillery Brigade, 1827.

Bombardier. 1st. Guards Artillery Brigade, 1828-1833.

776

Field-Grade Officer. 2nd Guards Artillery Brigade, 1828-1843.

777

Non-commissioned Officer [Feierverker] and Company-Grade Officer. 1st Guards Artillery Brigade, 1833-1843.

778

Company-Grade Officer and Drummer. 2nd Guards Artillery Brigade, 1833.

Company-Grade Officer and Bombardier. 6th Battery Battery of the 3rd Guards and Grenadier Artillery Brigade, 1833.

780

Company-Grade Officer. 3rd Light Battery of the 3rd Guards and Grenadier Artillery Brigade, 1833-1843.

781

Bombardier. Grenadier batteries of the 3rd Guards and Grenadier Artillery Brigade, 1834-1843.

782

Non-commissioned Officer [Feierverker]. 1st Guards Artillery Brigade, 1834-1843.

Drum-Major. 1st Guards Artillery Brigade, 1843-1844.

Company-Grade Officer, 1st Guards Artillery Brigade, and Drummer, 2nd Guards Artillery Brigade. 1844-1849.

785

Company-Grade Officer of the 6th Battery Battery, and Cannoneer and Company-Grade Officer of the 3rd Light Battery, 3rd Guards and Grenadier Artillery Brigade, 1844-1849.

Cannoneer. Guards Horse Artillery, 1827.

787

Non-commissioned Officer [Feierverker]. Guards Horse Artillery, 1828-1841.

788

Company-Grade Officer. Guards Horse Artillery, 1828-1843.

789

Cannoneer. Guards Horse Artillery, 1831-1855.

790

Bombardier. Guards Horse Artillery, 1835-1841.

791

Trumpeter. Guards Horse Artillery, 1836-1843.

792

Bombardier. Guards Horse Artillery, 1841-1843.

793

Company-Grade Officer. Guards Horse Artillery, 1843-1844.

Company-Grade Officer and Trumpeter. Guards Horse Artillery, 1844-1849.

795

General. Guards Horse Artillery, 1845-1849.

SOLDIERS, WEAPONS & UNIFORMS ALREADY PUBLISHED
(SOME TITLES)

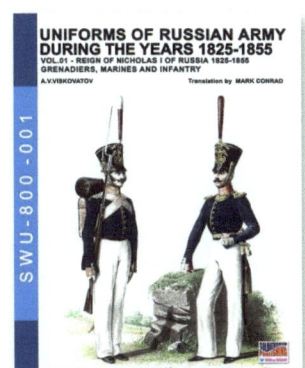
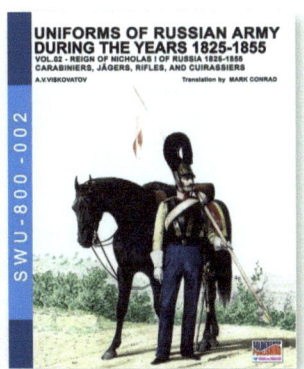
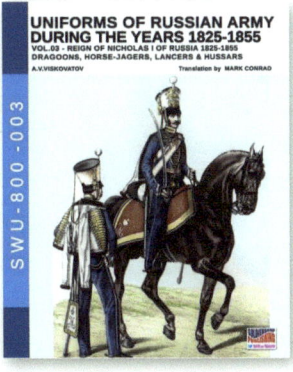
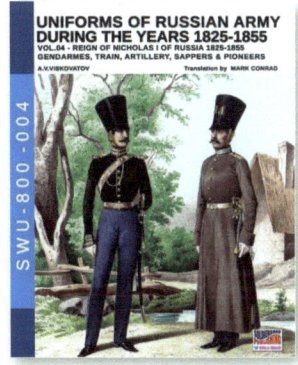
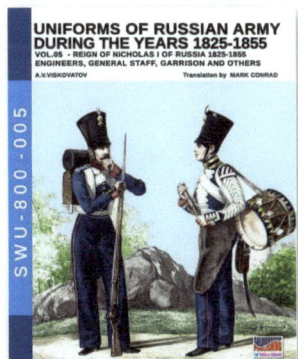
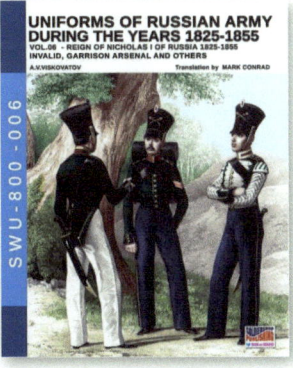
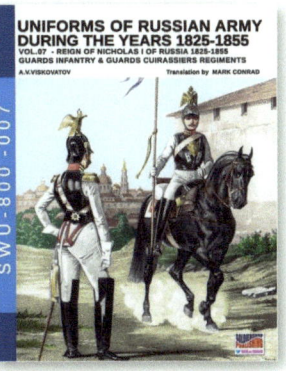
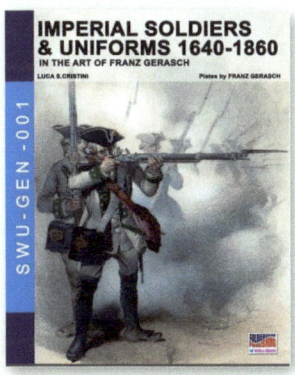
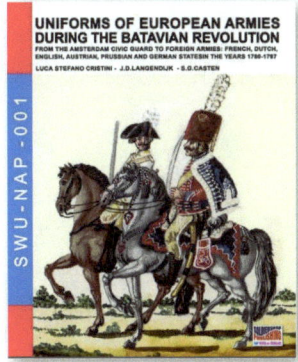
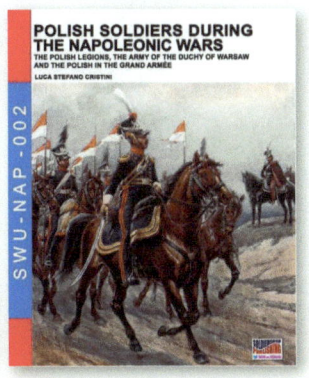
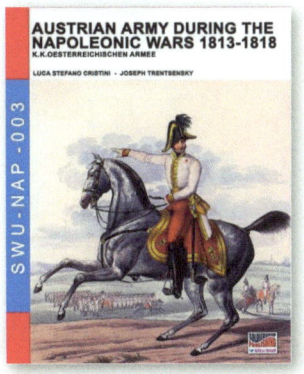
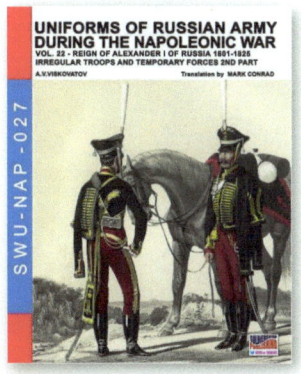
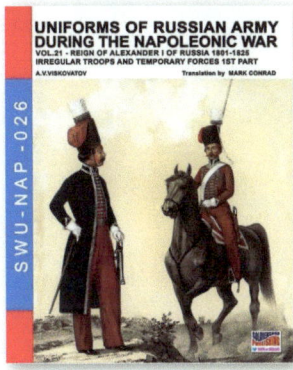
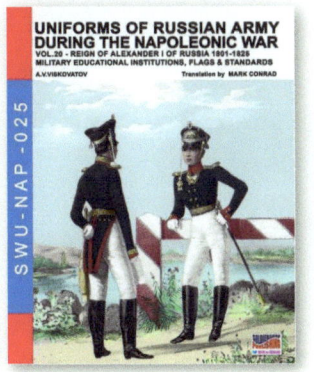
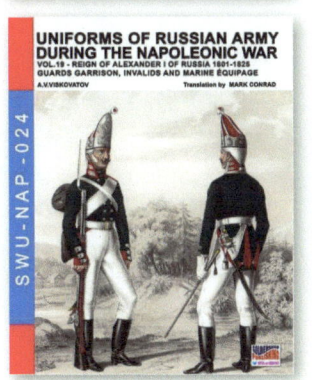
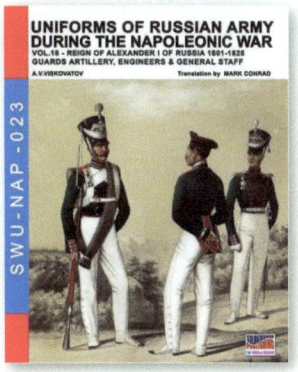

www.ingramcontent.com/pod-product-compliance
Lightning Source LLC
Chambersburg PA
CBHW041516220426
43668CB00003B/41